CACTUS THE ALL-AMERICAN PLANT

CACTUS

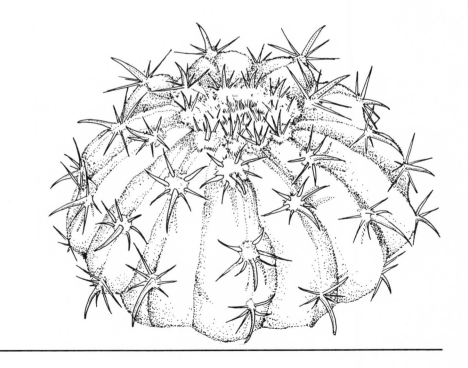

THE ALL-AMERICAN PLANT

by Anita Holmes

illustrated by Joyce Ann Powzyk

FOUR WINDS PRESS   NEW YORK

Grateful acknowledgment is made for the use of material from Cacti of the Southwest, Texas, New Mexico, Oklahoma, Arkansas, and Lousiana *by Del Weniger. © 1970 Del Weniger. Reproduced by permission of the University of Texas Press, Post Office Box 7819, Texas, 78812.*

J
635.9
H

Library of Congress Cataloging in Publication Data

Holmes, Anita (date)
    Cactus, the all-American plant.

    Bibliography: p.
    Includes index.
    SUMMARY: Describes cactus types, their environment, growth, uses, and home cultivation. Includes recipes and a list of desert gardens, museums, and natural areas of the Southwest where one may observe cacti.
    1. Cactus—Juvenile literature. 2. Botany—United States—Juvenile literature. [1. Cactus] I. Powzyk, Joyce. II. Title.
QK495.C11S59   635.9'3347   81–275
ISBN 0-590-07402-4   AACR1

Published by Four Winds Press. A division of Scholastic Inc., New York, N.Y. Text copyright © 1982 by Anita Holmes.   Illustrations copyright © 1982 by Scholastic Inc. All rights reserved. Printed in the United States of America. Library of Congress Catalog Card Number: 81-275.   1 2 3 4 5 86 85 84 83 82

ACKNOWLEDGMENTS

My thanks to the following people and institutions for contributing information and assistance: Eleanor Bell, Librarian, Norfolk Library, Norfolk, Connecticut; Eleanor Brown, El Paso, Texas; R. A. Countryman, Arizona Commission of Agriculture and Horticulture, Phoenix, Arizona; Carol D. Crosswhite, Boyce Thompson Southwestern Arboretum, Superior, Arizona; Laurence L. Hannafin, Norfolk, Connecticut; Jeff and Helen Ingram, Tucson, Arizona; Leo and Frances LaBelle, Phoenix, Arizona; Virginia F. Martin, The Cactus and Succulent Society of America, Arcadia, California; Leo J. Pickoff, Riverside, California; Miriam Ritzfield, Englewood, New Jersey; Louis P. Salamone, Norfolk, Connecticut; The Philip L. Boyd Deep Canyon Desert Research Center, University of California, Riverside, California; Huntington Library, San Marino, California; La Victoria Foods, Inc., Rosemead, California; National Museum of Natural History, Smithsonian Institution, Washington, D.C.; National Park Service, Saguaro

National Monument, Tucson, Arizona; and Organ Pipe Cactus National Monument, Ajo, Arizona; Rare Plant Studies Center, Austin, Texas.

Special thanks to Lyman Benson, Professor Emeritus, Department of Botany, Pomona College, Claremont, California, for answering many questions and offering encouragement; to Bettie Muckleroy, Houston, Texas, for allowing me to use information and recipes from her cooking column in the Houston Cactus and Succulent Society's monthly bulletin, *Kaktus Komments;* to Joyce L. Tate, Riverside, California, for answering questions about cactus cookery and supplying information and guidance; to my mother and father, for their interest and assistance; to my daughter, Juliette, for accompanying me on my forays into the desert and sharing my love for it; and to Gary Lyons, Horticulturist, Desert Garden, Huntington Botanical Gardens, San Marino, California, for reading the manuscript, suggesting changes, and supplying information and guidance.

How strange to realize then that this fantastic group of plants had never been seen by anyone in the so-called civilized world until after Columbus discovered America. Yet this must be true; for, except for two or three small, inconspicuous, and very uncactuslike species found in places even more unknown to early travelers in the jungles of Madagascar and Ceylon, the cacti grow naturally only in the Western Hemisphere. They are as American as corn, tomatoes, tobacco, or potatoes.

Del Weniger
Cacti of the Southwest

CONTENTS

INTRODUCTION

You probably learned in first or second grade that corn, tomatoes, tobacco, and potatoes were gifts to the Old World from the New World. These important plants had been cultivated by the Indians of the New World for centuries but were unknown to Europeans until Christopher Columbus discovered America.

Many other plants now grown all over the world belong to the New World as well. The cactus is one of these "all-American" plants.

Scientists believe the first cacti originated somewhere in Central or South America and then spread north and south throughout the Hemisphere. The early explorers found cacti growing on the dry plains of the Caribbean Islands. Cacti also occur naturally in many other habitats throughout the Americas. They grow on bleak, rocky mountain slopes, in open lava fields, along foggy coastal ledges, on sandy backbeaches, on windswept valleys, and on hardpacked gravel foothills. They even hang from trees in tropical forests.

We are fortunate to have over two hundred species of cacti growing within the United States. At least one species of cactus is native to each of our states except Hawaii, Alaska, Maine, Vermont, and New Hampshire. You can find them along our three coasts, on our grassy plains, and in our rocky mountains from Georgia to New York State. But, as you can guess, it is in the deserts of the Southwest where most of our cacti are found. (See map, p. 142.) The continual sunshine, the mineral-rich soil, and the mild winters of the Southwest are much to the liking of a host of cacti.

Thousands of tourists flock to the Southwest each year to see its natural wonders. Carlsbad Caverns, the Petrified Forest, and the Grand Canyon are fantastic sights which attract large numbers of people. But none is more fantastic than the cacti which grow in the region. Spiny and oddly shaped, cacti are natural wonders in their own right.

I grew up in southern California and Texas, two states where cacti are common. I had taken cacti for granted the way people in the East take maple and birch trees for granted and people in the South take no notice of pine trees and honeysuckle. I had picked their fruit and been pricked by some, but otherwise I paid little attention to the plants.

Later I developed an interest in exotic plants and discovered that cacti are among the most unusual and exotic plants on earth. Plant lovers from around the world come to our Southwest just to study and examine these plants.

Unfortunately, it is not as easy to find some of our rare cacti as it was one hundred years ago. The American Southwest is changing. Lands there are developing rapidly. Cities are expanding. Land once open is being used for farming and agriculture. Scientists fear that a number of cacti are in danger of extinction.

My interest in cacti and my concern for them led me to write this book. Writing a book is a great excuse to learn more about a topic that interests you. This book has been just that—an excuse to study these fascinating New World plants more fully and an excuse to travel back to cactus country to renew my acquaintance with them. It is my hope that this book will in some way kindle a regard in you, the reader, for these sometimes strange but more often beautiful and always fascinating plants.

It would be difficult in one small book to discuss all the species of cacti or even all the places that cacti grow. While the major cactus groups are mentioned in this book, I have discussed most fully those cacti found in the hot deserts of the American Southwest. Arizona's Sonoran Desert is one of the best places in the United States to study cacti. It is a cactus lover's paradise, where cacti reach the size of trees and dominate the land.

ANITA HOLMES
SHARON, CONNECTICUT

CHAPTER ONE

Into Cactus Country

Landscape in cactus country

The train rumbled along as it had all night. I lay in my pull-down bed jostling with each rocking movement. I was trying hard to stay asleep. Something was disturbing me, nagging at my sleepiness. I rolled over and thrust my face more deeply into the pillow. A few more moments of sleep, then. . . . There it was again. I opened one eye. Zap. It got me.

The desert sun is bright and penetrating. Even early in the morning it shines with the brilliance of a midday sun. Its insistent rays had squeezed in underneath my window shade. There was no avoiding it.

I sat up in the narrow bed and rolled up the window shade. A world of scrubby bushes, cacti, rocky hills, and mesquite trees said hello. We were on the high plateaus of west Texas at the edge of the Chihuahuan Desert. It had taken me three days by train to get here. I was terribly pleased that old Mr. Sun had been able to awaken me.

My trip had begun in New York City where I purchased a ticket for Tucson, Arizona, an excellent base from which to visit points of interest within the Sonoran Desert. I boarded the Southern Railroad and traveled some 1,400 miles south to New Orleans, Louisiana. There my train connected with the Sunset Limited, which goes west.

You go through a lot of different kinds of country on a trip through the United States. It is interesting to watch the landscape change as the train moves from north to south and from east to west. The effect land and climate have on plants can be startling.

MOVING SOUTH Between New York and New Orleans you pass through miles of woods and farmland. The woods and forests of the Atlantic seaboard are a thickly overgrown mixture of tall deciduous and evergreen trees, with smaller varieties underneath. Along the railroad tracks, creeping vines such as honeysuckle and greenbrier cover trees, shrubs, fences—anything they can. Everything is green, and crowded, and tangled. It is obvious that water is plentiful and there is enough for keeping any number of plants alive. Unlike the desert, you rarely see the bare earth except where someone has plowed. Low places where water collects are full of briars and swamp or marsh plants.

The land drops and becomes swampy as one approaches the Gulf of Mexico. Outside of New Orleans water-loving trees such as cypress are overgrown with moss and draped with vines. In marshes grasses stand in shallow waters. Again there is no bare soil.

MOVING WEST New Orleans and most of the coastal South are flat. The land west of that coastal city continues flat and grassy and wet into east Texas. Occasionally the flatness is interrupted by a hillock of woods. Then it starts getting drier. Marsh and swamp become flat grassland. The farther west into Texas you go, the farther from moist ocean winds, the drier the land becomes.

At some point the land begins to rise—first to five hundred feet and finally to one thousand and two thousand feet. As the land rises, it gets even drier. Near San Antonio, in the Texas hill country, rocks jut up from grassy, scrubby, and wooded land. Cacti and other desert plants begin mixing with the grasses and trees. By the time you reach the high plateaus of west Texas, grassland has given over to bone-dry land. You have reached the edge of the Chihuahuan Desert. This desert makes up a large part of central Mexico and pokes a few fingers into Texas, New Mexico, and Arizona.

We hit the Chihuahuan Desert about 5:30 in the morning. What a dry, desolate, and dazzling sight it was. Miles and miles of brown earth, rocky outcroppings, and scraggly dryland plants lay stretched out under a huge, blue sky. There were no signs of people anywhere.

I spotted a clump of yellow-blossomed, oval-padded prickly pears. Looking as if a juggler had arranged them, they are a series of spiny pancakelike stems, one balanced upon another. Huge clumps of these many-jointed plants dotted the brown, sunbaked landscape.

Prickly pear fruit

Though some species of prickly pear are endangered, these of the Chihuahuan Desert are not. In fact they have taken over areas where cattle have destroyed the natural grasses. Even so, I was thrilled to see these familiar plants of my childhood. My father had taught me to eat their sweet prickly fruit, called pears (or tunas). We would knock off

The Chihuahuan Desert

the spines, peel the skin back, and then bite into the seed-filled pulp.
If we weren't careful, the red juice would run down our hands and
arms, staining our clothes.

The train sounded its horn and a jackrabbit bolted from a hideout
under a scraggly bush near the tracks to a quieter spot beneath a prickly
pear some thirty feet away. Farther on some grazing cattle looked up.
They prefer the grasses that grow thickest on the rocky hills which rise
up from the desert plateau, but when grass is scarce, they will turn to
shrubs and the spiny pads of the prickly pear. I remembered a story
a rancher uncle of mine told of how during severe droughts, when grass
was scarce, he used to singe the spines off these very plants so that his
cattle would not starve:

Mixed with the prickly pears here were mesquite trees, creosote bush, sage, and other low bushes and shrubs, and two common plants of the Chihuahuan Desert, yuccas and ocotillos. The spiny, whip-shape branches of the ocotillo are often mistaken for cacti as are the fibrous, sword-shape leaves of the yucca. Neither is a cactus at all. They are similar though in that they have learned to live in the dry deserts where the sun burns hot most of the year.

I had moved from my own sitting room to a comfortable spot in the lounge car. A girl had been told that you could often spot deer from the train in the morning. No sooner had I sat down than she exclaimed to her mother, "Look, over there." A large deer stood in startled stillness as our train rumbled heavily by.

The morning advanced rapidly. Miles of desert followed miles of more desert. Occasionally a town would appear on the desert horizon. We would approach it, pass through it, and leave it as quickly as we had come.

By midafternoon we had crossed west Texas and were approaching El Paso. This Texas city lies at the Texas-New Mexico border. Here the desert stands against a backdrop of jagged brown mountains.

I had the chance to talk to the brakeman. He had lived in the area all of his life, and I asked him if he liked the desert. "It's the only thing I know," he said. "Yes, I like it. But it's cruel. Nothing but rattlesnakes and coyotes out there."

Many people call the desert cruel. The brakeman was exaggerating when he said there was nothing but rattlesnakes and coyotes in the desert. But was he right to call it cruel? Certainly its plants are spiny and its heat severe. And a desert is no place to be caught in a windstorm or torrential rain. The blowing sand lashes your skin raw in the one, and when rain comes, it often causes flash floods which can wash you away if you're in a low spot.

On the other hand, there is a sunny peace in the way plants grow apart in the desert, as if a master gardener placed each one by hand. Coyotes do not trouble people, and as for rattlesnakes, they are not really a problem. You can always see where you are putting your feet. I find a tropical forest or a swamp much more threatening in this respect. You can never see what is underfoot.

Inside New Mexico, we crossed a dry stream bed called an *arroyo*. A piglike creature called a *javelina,* or peccary, trotted away from our train. He did not seem to find the desert cruel. He was at his ease, probably looking for a prickly pear on which to munch.

Perhaps the desert seems cruel to those who try to make something out of it which it isn't. To its natives—the plants and animals that have lived in it for ages and made their peace with it—it is not cruel.

By late afternoon, we were leaving the Chihuahuan Desert and approaching the Sonoran. Many of the plants found in the Chihuahuan

are here as well. The Sonoran Desert makes up a large portion of Central Arizona and westcentral Mexico.

Javelina in an arroyo

As we left New Mexico and crossed into Arizona, I spotted a stand of barrel cacti. These plants, perhaps one-and-a-half feet tall, were situated on a rocky slope each a few feet from one another, just as a stand of trees in another area might grow on a similar slope. They were impressive and offered a preview of the sights to come.

Barrel cactus

We had been traveling across the desert for some twelve hours now and would soon be in Tucson. Darkness was beginning to fall. My eyes flitted everywhere, trying to search out the shape of other cacti. I was looking for a saguaro, Arizona's state plant and the largest of our cacti. But as we neared the desert city, I could no longer see the desert floor. The lights of highways, streets, and buildings glared in my eyes. I would have to wait until morning to see the spectacular sights of the Sonoran Desert.

CHAPTER TWO

Adapted to a Hard Life

Pediocactus peeblesianus

The city of Tucson lies spread out in a flat desert valley in southern Arizona. It is surrounded by jagged mountains which loom brown and blue and purple on the horizon. Houses and lawns and stores and roads have pretty much replaced the natural desert on the valley floor. But as you leave the town and approach the mountain foothills, you meet the Sonoran Desert much as it must have been before the white man settled here.

I rented a car and drove to a section of the Saguaro National Monument that borders Tucson to the west. A national monument is an area that has been preserved for its historical or scientific importance. Saguaro National Monument was established in 1933 as a preserve for the mighty, tree-size saguaro cacti, the largest plants of the Sonoran Desert. Some very old stands of these giant plants lie within the monument.

As I reached the crest of the Tucson Mountains, I could see the monument stretched out beneath me. It was all that I had expected— a fantastic, shadeless forest where spiny plants of all shapes and sizes were collected under the towering, leafless branches of the saguaros. Creosote bushes, ocotillos, and sage were here as well as familiar prickly pears, barrel, and other cacti. There were tall cacti, fat and skinny ones, large ones and small ones, ones that stood erect and others that rambled along the ground. Some had one stem, others had many. They grew in all kinds of places—along the bottoms of the rocky mountain slopes called *bajadas;* in flat, open areas; among boulders; in hardpacked sand and gravel; alone; and in groups.

I parked the car and walked among the plants. Beneath the saguaros, which stood like giant sentries along the mountain slopes, I felt small and insignificant and a little awed. It is common for a mature saguaro to grow over forty feet high. A few reach fifty feet, the height of a five-story building. They dwarf everything around them. One look at their scarred bodies and I could see that they had been on earth a long time and had endured many hardships. A few had been standing when the Revolutionary War was occupying George Washington and

The Sonoran Desert

his troops in the East. Many more had witnessed the opening of the West and had seen the first miners search the desert for land and riches.

I examined several of the cholla scattered about the monument. These cacti, close relatives of the prickly pears, have narrow, cylindrical stems which are very spiny. I steered clear of the "jumping chollas." Being very brittle, the stems of these cacti will break off at the slightest touch. As the spines are strong enough to puncture a tire, you can imagine how painful running into one could be.

A "jumping cholla"

I kept to the barren areas between plants. Composed of hardpacked dirt and stone, these areas tended to run in curving paths down the mountain slopes like well-worn country roads. By keeping a sharp eye, I discovered small varieties of cacti hunkered down among the rocks. Ground-hugging hedgehog cacti dwarfed beneath the tall majesty of the larger cacti formed agreeable clumps of green.

A hedgehog cactus

The morning went by quickly. The sun got hotter and hotter. By noon the thermometer read over 100 degrees Fahrenheit. I began to feel the need of some shade and a cooling drink. As I walked toward the car, it struck me that the desert plants were a lot hardier than I was. All deserts are dry. The Sonoran is hot as well. I could take the desert's heat for only a few hours at a time, and yet day after day, week after week, the desert cacti, trees, and shrubs went about the business of living without any relief from the sun and without so much as a drop of rain.

How do they do it? Some, like the creosote bush, drop their leaves during the driest seasons and become dormant much as an oak or maple tree does in winter. Some, such as the desert wild flowers, bloom for a brief period when moisture is available and then die, leaving their seeds to repeat the process the next year. Others, such as the mesquite tree, send a long root into the earth to tap the water that lies deep below. Still others store water within their stems or leaves and draw upon it when needed. Such plants are called succulents. *Cacti are succulents*. The ability of cacti to withstand long periods of drought is one of nature's great success stories.

Cactus History

Cacti are among the youngest plants on earth. Their ancestors may date back no farther than twenty to forty million years ago. To us, this sounds old. But by comparison, the first land plants probably developed some 400 million years ago, and the first of the flowering plants, about 130 million years ago.

No one knows where the first cacti developed or what they looked like. No fossil cacti have been found to offer clues. Scientists assume that cacti originated somewhere in the central part of the Western Hemisphere, perhaps in Mexico, equatorial South America, or the West Indies.

The theory goes that the first cacti were probably very much like ordinary green plants. They had green leaves and woody stems and they required plenty of moisture. They may have inhabited grassy and forested areas and perhaps even the edges of marshes. Scientists believe they may have been relatives of the citrus family of plants, or perhaps the myrtle family.

A pereskia stem

Over the centuries, the environment around them began to change. Weather, soil, even the shape of the land changed. Massive earth movements tilted islands and created mountains where none had been before. Some areas were cut off from winds which previously had carried moist air and rains from the oceans. These cut-off areas became hotter and drier. The plants that depended on a lot of moisture began dying off. Those that—through one mechanism or another—could get along on less survived. Time went on and the process continued. The land got drier, more plants died out, and a few got tougher. Of those that survived, one kind had developed that could live on stored water for long periods. It had thick woody stems; thick waxy leaves; spines; green bark which could manufacture food; and a mass of roots that could soak up water fast.

Some plants like this exist today. They are an ancient kind of cactus called pereskias. Scientists believe these plants are the direct descendants of the first cacti. From the pereskia type, other cacti developed which differed even more from common green plants. Some literally reshaped themselves in order to survive in the changing environment.

HOW THEY SURVIVED

COLLECTING WATER If you lived where it rarely rained, how do you suppose you would get water? Perhaps you would design a way of collecting a lot of water when it did rain. Perhaps you would build a catch basin that covered a large area. Maybe you would build canals and channels to feed water into the basin.

The typical cactus functions in just this way. Most cacti have widespread roots which can absorb a lot of water quickly from a wide area. The roots of a mature saguaro may spread out in a fifty-foot circle around the plant. These roots grow close to the soil's surface enabling the plants to take in water no matter how brief the rain or how quickly it passes through the soil.

Typical cactus root system

Wide spreading

Shallow

A few cacti are supported by tuberous roots. Looking like huge sweet potatoes or turnips, these roots are filled with a spongy pulp which holds water. During drought the plants rely on this water for their survival.

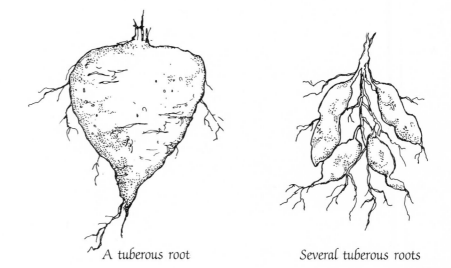

A tuberous root   Several tuberous roots

When the Rains Come

Rain falls upon the Sonoran Desert during two seasons a year. A brief rainy season in winter is followed by a long dry spring. Then in July or August the rains come again.

First the sky darkens over the vast desert as large clouds move down from the rocky mountains and blot out the burning summer sun. Lightning flashes across the sky in long jagged bolts. Thunder shakes the earth and the air cools. Finally, raindrops as big as quarters splatter against the desert's dry floor, sending mud a foot into the air and creating rivulets which swell into tiny streams and finally into raging rivers.

The waiting cacti respond to the pounding rain as if by magic. Triggered by the welcomed moisture, special rain roots sprout to help take in the water. Their millions of tiny root cells begin gulping water as fast as their water-pumping mechanisms can work. From one cell to the next, water is sent up to the waiting stems and branches above.

STORING WATER A cactus can be tall and columnar like a saguaro or globose like a barrel cactus. It can be flat jointed like a prickly pear or cylindrical jointed like a cholla. It can be subglobose or ovoid. These words describe the shapes of cactus stems. (See pp. 18–19.)

Whatever its shape, a cactus stem is usually thick. Cacti developed thick stems and branches in order to store water. The stems are filled with a spongy pulp which can hold vast amounts of water. As the plant takes in the water, the pulp swells up, just as a sponge does when dropped in a pail of water. During the long months of drought that may follow a period of rain, the plants draw on their water reserves. As the water is used, the pulp shrinks and the plant begins to shrivel. It will fill out again during the next rainy season.

A giant saguaro may weigh as much as five tons when filled with water. During a long drought it may lose half its weight in water. As you can imagine, all the expanding and filling and shriveling and shrinking that goes on within the plant over the course of its life puts stress on its skin. This explains why the saguaro and so many other desert cacti are pleated or warty. The deep-pleated surface of a saguaro can fold and unfold like an accordion as it takes in and uses up water.

How could a five-ton, water-filled sponge stand up like a tree? Nature has given the saguaro and most of the large, treelike cacti reinforcements. Woody interior ribs act as support beams. They run the length of the plant helping to hold it erect. The plant's water-storing tissue encircles these ribs.

CONSERVING WATER Anybody who has spent time in the desert knows it is important to ration water. Wasting water could mean the difference between survival and death. Cacti have developed many ways to conserve water. They are water misers of the highest order.

Saguaro ribs and interior

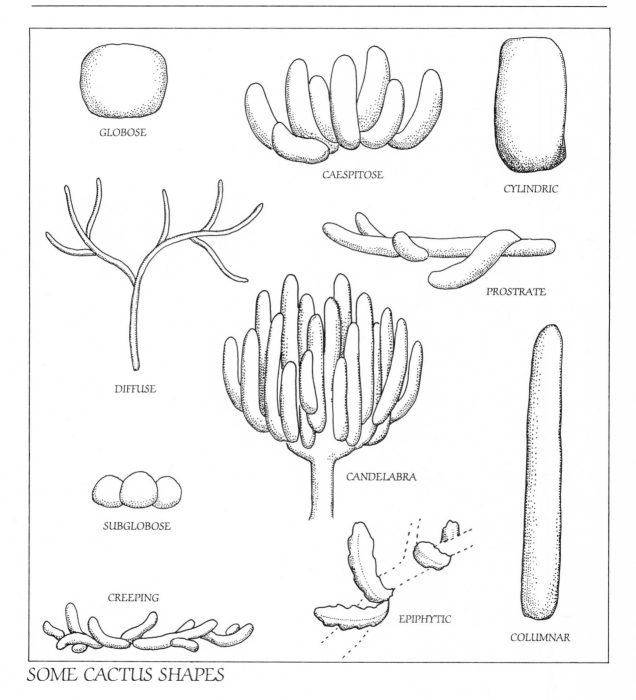

GLOBOSE

CAESPITOSE

CYLINDRIC

DIFFUSE

PROSTRATE

CANDELABRA

SUBGLOBOSE

COLUMNAR

CREEPING

EPIPHYTIC

SOME CACTUS SHAPES

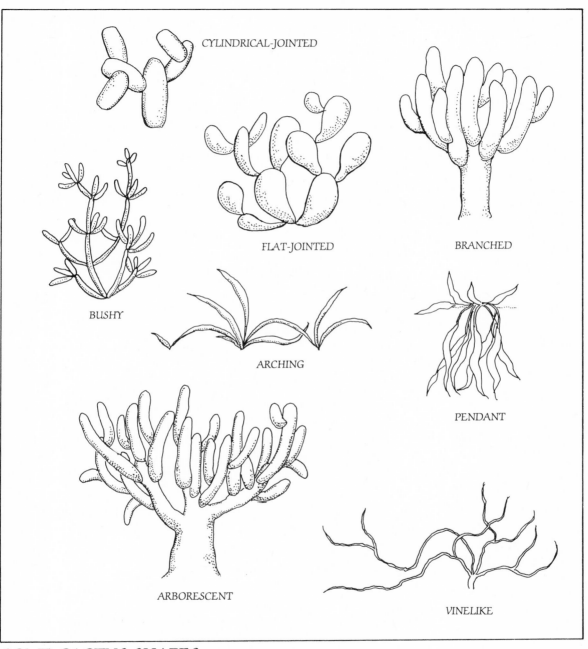

CYLINDRICAL-JOINTED

FLAT-JOINTED

BRANCHED

BUSHY

ARCHING

PENDANT

ARBORESCENT

VINELIKE

SOME CACTUS SHAPES

NO LEAVES All green plants use water in manufacturing food. It is in water that the dissolved mineral nutrients from the soil are carried into the plant. As the nutrients are converted into the plant's food, the water becomes waste which must be disposed of. The plant gets rid of the extra water through transpiration. The water is transpired (breathed out) through stomata, the pores in the plant's leaves.

Take a look at the cacti and cactus shapes pictured so far in this book. Notice that except for the ancient pereskia cactus (shown on p. 14), each is leafless.

Leaves provide a plant with a large surface from which to transpire water. This large, leafy surface makes it possible for a plant to take in and transpire water rapidly. For plants with a good water supply, this is a benefit. Fast transpiration means fast growth. The faster nutrients are brought into the plant, the faster it will grow.

Cacti have sacrificed fast growth for survival. They have abandoned leaves in order to reduce the rate at which they lose water. An oak tree may transpire as much as six hundred quarts of water in a single day. A small palm might transpire five hundred quarts. A twelve-foot saguaro gets along on as little as *one-fifteenth of one quart of water* in the same period. Drought-resistant cacti use much less water than green leafy plants. A leafy plant releases about six thousand times more water in a given period of time than a cactus plant of the same weight.

How can cacti get along without leaves as it is in the leaves that most green plants manufacture food? The color of their stems offers a clue. Cacti stems contain the important food-making substance, chlorophyll, which is found in the leaves of most other green plants. The work of manufacturing food is carried out in these stems.

A stomata

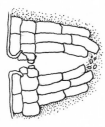

The stomata, the little pores through which plants transpire, are also located in the stems. Relative to other plants, these are few and far apart. The reduction in the number of pores through which moisture escapes helps to slow down transpiration.

INSULATING SKIN The skin of a cactus is like that of a watermelon or cucumber—waxy. Its waxy coating helps to keep moisture in by insulating the plant, much as a plastic bag around a head of lettuce keeps its leaves crisp and water filled.

BUMPS AND SPINES The ribbed or warty surfaces of many cacti allow them to store and release water effectively. These irregular surfaces plus heavy spine coverings also seem to limit water loss. The deep pleats on a saguaro and the bumps on a cholla deflect light away from the plant. Thus the underparts of the stems are shaded from direct light. The protective spines, bristles, and hairs found on most cacti also screen the sun's rays. It is estimated that spines reduce the sun's intensity by as much as 20 percent in some cacti.

In addition the spines counteract the drying effect of the wind by slowing down the rate at which it whips around the plants. Hot, dry winds can absorb a lot of moisture and quickly dry out a plant. By breaking the force of the wind, the rate at which moisture is carried away is slowed. If you have tried to grow a potted plant over a radiator, you know how quickly hot, moving air dries out plants and soil.

THICK SAP Within Saguaro National Monument I came across numerous woody skeletons—the ribbed remains of saguaros and other cylindrical cacti. One skeleton was still standing. At a distance it seemed to be oozing sap. The substance glistened in the sun. Expecting to find it wet, I ran my finger over it. It was dry and slick and hard. The desert winds had done their job of robbing the last drops of moisture from the dying giant. But it had taken a long time. The moisture inside a cactus is trapped in a thick, syrupy sap which does not readily release the moisture.

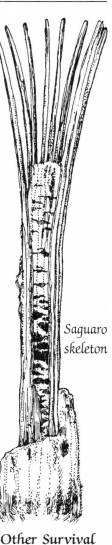

Saguaro skeleton

Other Survival Measures

As you can see, the cactus has developed an elaborate system for storing and conserving water. In part, this has left it open to other dangers.

Its widespread root system enables it to collect water from a large area. At the same time these roots tend to discourage other plants from growing close. Though prickly pears and chollas often form huge thickets, most cacti grow alone surrounded by nothing more than dry dirt and desert stones. Standing alone this way, each can easily fall prey to one of the many hungry or thirsty animals that inhabit the desert. Is it any wonder then that the cactus has armed itself with spines? Without its protective spines, the cacti may not have survived as a plant family.

Some cacti have other ways to discourage animal attack. Some contain an unappetizing sap. Others are well camouflaged. Their color or shape help them to blend into their surroundings and remain unnoticed. One group of cacti called Living Rocks are so unplantlike in appearance that they are easily overlooked. (See pp. 84–85.)

Survival of the Species

Without thinking about it or even caring, all members of the plant world are involved in the work to continue their race. It is one of the great wonders of nature that each living thing leaves something of itself behind so that the species can continue.

In the case of flowering plants, of course, seeds are left behind to become new plants. But seeds require moisture in order to sprout. The seed of a cactus has to be as hardy as the plant itself to withstand the long periods of drought in a desert.

The typical desert cactus seed can survive two, three, even fifteen years of desert heat and drought. Most will not try to sprout until conditions are right. They will wait for several springs if necessary until one promises enough moisture to promote growth.

During the long periods while the seeds lie in wait, they face many dangers. Rodents, birds, ants, and the like may eat them. They may be carried away by water or wind. Here again most cacti have some insurance. Most produce an amazing number of seeds. This insures that at least some of the seeds will survive until sprouting time. A saguaro produces forty to fifty million seeds during its life just to assure that three or four will succeed in becoming adult plants.

A few cacti like the chollas propagate themselves vegetatively. A segment of stem falls to the ground and takes root. In time it becomes a new plant just like its parent. The broken plant segments need moisture and warmth in order to root. The natural succulence of the cactus stem and its waxy skin enable the segment to remain alive until enough moisture is available for rooting.

A typical young cactus growing under the shade of desert brush

CHAPTER THREE

Each Plays Its Part

Astrophytum asterias

In nature every plant and every animal plays a role in its environment. The tall trees of a forest serve by providing homes, feeding places, and refuge to many woodland creatures. Birds, squirrels, and insects feed and nest in their trunks and branches. Other animals climb them for safety. In their shade smaller trees, shrubs, ferns, wildflowers, mushrooms, mosses, and the like form a moist haven for ground-dwelling animals.

Likewise, the larger cacti play an important role in the desert. Over centuries of adaptation, the cacti developed the ability to withstand drought and other hardships. Having solved the problem of desert living, they then made it possible for less hardy forms of life to survive in the desert as well. Like their leafy forest counterparts, the saguaros and other large cacti serve as homes, feeding stations, and shelter to dozens of desert animals.

Upon a Saguaro It takes no more than a few hours around the saguaros to see why they are often called the desert's high-rise apartments. From the tops of their branches to the base of their long trunks, these giant cacti attract animals day and night.

One morning I got up just as the sun was sending a yellowish pink glow over the desert floor. It was cool with a slight hint of moisture in the air. I hopped in my car and headed for the desert foothills. Not far from the road I noticed a large nest of sticks and twigs positioned among the high arms of one of the tall saguaros. I got out of my car to get a closer look just in time to see what had been occupying this penthouse apartment. With a great flapping of wings a large red-tailed hawk rose off the nest and began soaring in a great circle overhead. The hawk is only one of several large birds that enjoy the views from atop the giant saguaros and use them as lookouts, launching pads, and homes for their families.

As I stood waiting to see if the bird would return to its nest, I noticed that lower down in the same saguaro were numerous fist-size holes. Surely some living thing had made those holes. Was it inside?

If you live in a city you undoubtedly know what a building su-

A hawk landing on nest atop a saguaro

perintendent is. The "super" is the person who takes care of the building and handles any problems the tenants might have. The super can handle repair jobs and often is an accomplished carpenter and painter.

The saguaros come staffed with two building superintendents, both excellent carpenters. Both are woodpeckers and both keep the saguaros pest free and spotted with clean, comfortable apartments.

The Gila woodpecker, a nine-inch bird with black and white striped wings and tail and a bright red cap on its crown, builds and tends to all the apartments above fourteen feet high. Mearns gilded flicker, a larger bird with brown wings and a yellow breast and tail, is super for the lower stories, those below fourteen feet. During the spring the desert silence is frequently broken with a rat-a-tat-tat as the birds work with their ice-picklike beaks to break through the tough skin of the saguaro and peck out holes for nesting.

The holes are round on the outside, perhaps three to four inches in diameter. Inside they are gourd-shape. The birds first dig out an entrance tunnel and then bore downward to form a longish pocket about the size of a football. The walls of the pockets are dry and smooth and cool, not at all moist and gooey as you might expect. When a saguaro is punctured, its oozing sap hardens and seals the wound much as our bodies create scabs to seal our wounds and keep us from bleeding to death. The crust is so durable that even after the plant dies and its succulent stem has withered away, the cavities remain intact. Desert Indians used these cavities as drinking vessels.

As retreats from the desert's heat, woodpecker nests are unsurpassed. Any visitor to the desert quickly learns that not only is the air temperature hot there, the ground gets extremely hot as well. With few clouds to reflect the sun's rays back into the atmosphere, the desert is like a huge solar collector. Most of the sun's energy reaches the desert floor and is absorbed by it. This means that on a summer's day the desert soil may be 50 degrees Fahrenheit hotter than the air above it. Cacti have adapted to these hot conditions, but people and most desert animals have not. Most animals must spend the hottest part of the day "holed up" to escape the heat. Some burrow underground. Some rest in the shade of plants, rocks, or caves. Others retreat to a cactus.

Gila woodpecker   *Gilded flicker*

Tests have shown that the air inside a woodpecker hole can be 20 degrees to 25 degrees cooler than the outside air during the day and as much as 12 degrees warmer at night. The thick moist trunk of the saguaro and the protective crust which forms the wall of the nest are effective insulators.

The gilas and the gildeds peck out numerous holes during their lifetimes, at least one each spring and usually more. The holes they abandon can be used by other animals. In the main the animals that nest in these holes have greater luck in raising their young than animals that nest on the open desert floor.

Brown bats, packrats, mice, and insects are among the nonbird users of the holes. And at least sixteen species of birds use saguaro holes abandoned or left unguarded by the accommodating woodpeckers. Among them are western kingbirds, English sparrows, house finches,

A woodpecker hole in a saguaro

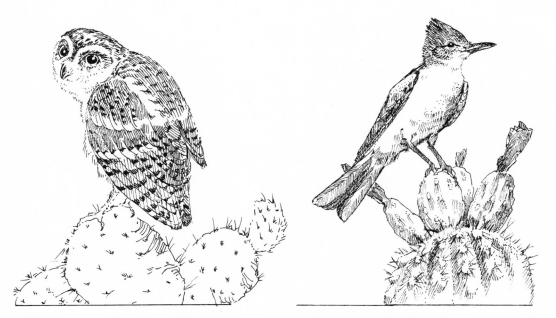

Elf owl   *Arizona crested flycatcher*

and several owls. Three species nest almost exclusively in these saguaro apartments and would be in trouble without them—the Arizona crested flycatcher, the saguaro or Mexican screech owl, and the world's smallest owl, the elf owl. The owls, of course, are nocturnal and are rarely seen in daytime.

No matter what other role they may play, green plants form the base of nature's food chain. Beginning with green plants, nutrients are passed from one living thing to another. Plant eaters feed upon green plants. They in turn may become food for animal eaters. Without the green plants to manufacture food from air, water, and soil, the plant eaters and the animal eaters would go hungry.

Cactus fruits, seeds, and stems provide food and moisture for many desert animals. So do their flowers which contain nourishing nectar and pollen. Being green and succulent the year long, cactus stems, too, are an important source of food and water especially during drought, when water is scarce and other food sources have dried up.

Throughout the day in spring and summer there is a hustle and bustle around the saguaros as many animals come to feed upon them. Though as many as 70 percent of the desert animals spend the hot days of spring and summer hiding from the burning rays of the sun, this still leaves 30 percent moving about. Most of this daytime activity involves birds and insects. The ability to fly allows these animals to rise above the extreme heat of the earth's surface and keep busy through all but the hottest parts of the day.

The attractive white blossoms that sit upon the tips of the saguaro's branches, like perky women's hats, attract bees, wasps, flies, butterflies, and of course, birds. The two apartment builders, along with mourning doves and others, enjoy this sweet nectar and can be seen dipping their beaks into the yellow centers in a dip-lift-drink type of rhythm. When the saguaro fruits ripen, they, too, are visited by numerous birds and insects. White-wing doves visit the desert briefly each year at saguaro-blossoming time. First they feed on the saguaro nectar and then on the saguaro fruits. (See p. 50.) For these periods their normally pale breasts first take on the yellow cast of the saguaro pollen and then are dyed crimson from the juice of the deep red fruits.

Saguaro flower

When the fruits fall, hosts of ground dwellers are able to feast upon their sweet red flesh. At dusk and during the night various rodents, javelina, deer, coyotes, and the like join spiders, ants, beetles, lizards, and turtles in enjoying the tasty treats. The black seeds are consumed by various birds and rodents.

Saguaro stems themselves offer nourishment and moisture and they often harbor insects that are of interest to many creatures. Woodpeckers in particular have a great taste for the cactus beetle whose larvae bore into saguaros.

Some animals come to the saguaros to hunt. I never saw either, but two desert snakes, the racer snake and the gopher snake, will often brave the prickly saguaro spines in search of young birds nested in the holes above.

Day and night around the saguaros

*Among
the Chollas
and
Prickly Pears*

One day I visited the Southwest Arboretum, thirty miles or so outside Phoenix. It is a botanical garden where you can see cacti and other desert plants from all over the world. Surrounding the formal plantings is open desert and a few marked trails where you can learn about the natural vegetation of the Sonoran Desert. I was lucky enough to get a guided tour from the Arboretum's naturalist, a woman who knew a great deal about desert plants and desert ecology.

Birds were singing noisily in the branches of the mesquite and palo verde trees and darting back and forth from tall cactus to tall cactus. It was not especially hot for the desert, only 98 degrees Fahrenheit, and the desert floor was alive with the zip and skid of some of the desert's small lizards that run so fast they are little more than a blur as they whip by you.

We were walking along through a stand of prickly pears and chollas, admiring the desert and talking about the animals that live in it, when a flutter of wings right at my shoulder startled me and drew my attention to an aged cholla nearby. The flap of wings had been a cactus wren, the largest wren in the United States and the state bird of Arizona. We had scared the spotted brown bird off its nest, which was tucked in among the spiniest branches of the plant. Upon examination I found the nest to be the most perfectly built one I had ever seen. It was an envelope of twigs lined with feathers and soft grasses, and smaller twigs. The entrance was neat and cylindrical and encircled with the protective spines of the cholla. My guide pointed out other large chollas. Nearly every one had several nests either tucked in among its spiny branches or resting on top. Cactus wrens, curve-billed thrashers, verdins, mourning doves, black-throated sparrows, purple martins, and even the large and humorous mascots of the desert, roadrunners, have discovered the advantages of building homes within the spiniest recesses of these spiniest of all cacti. The plants also offer to the desert's animals nectar and pollen in the spring, fruit in the summer, and seeds into the fall, just as the saguaros do.

Farther on we passed a low-sprawling prickly pear. Several of its pads had been nibbled by some desert creature and were now decorated with the scallops of its hungry bites.

Cactus wren near nest in a cholla

My guide pointed to the nibbled pads. "Can you guess what has been feeding here?" she asked.

"No," I said.

"A packrat. Its den is less than six feet away. See if you can find it."

Rising to the challenge, I searched the area. I could not see anything that looked very formal, nothing as neat as a bird's nest or as obvious as a beaver's lodge. But atop the sprawling cactus was an unkempt mound of twigs surrounded with spiny cholla joints.

"Could that be it?" I said, not at all sure I was even looking at anything animal-made.

A packrat nest under
a prickly pear

It was. The mound was about two feet high and maybe four or five feet across at the base. It had obviously been built with the sole intent of keeping out unwanted visitors.

The naturalist told me that the mound of debris represented the animal's fortress and discouraged entry to its living quarters which were below. These consisted of a network of underground passages and chambers.

The packrat, also known as a trade rat, wood rat, or Neotoma, is not a rat at all but a clean little rodent with big ears and bushy whiskers. Neither its mouth nor its small feet are armor plated, yet it is able to run over the spiny chollas and carry their joints in its mouth without any difficulty. It lines the entrances to its chambers with the joints to keep out predators and then lines its chambers with softer and smoother materials—small twigs, feathers, grasses, shredded bark, whatever is about. Sometimes this includes man-made objects dropped or left unguarded by desert visitors. It is not unusual to find jewelry, ballpoint pens, bits of cloth—anything portable—within the nest of a packrat. You can see where it gets its name.

Perhaps of all the creatures in the desert the packrat relies on cacti most heavily. Not only does it nest among them and use their spiny joints and branches for protection, but about 44 percent of its diet is cacti. It consumes stems, seeds, and fruits when available. During times of drought it may get as much as 90 percent of its food from cacti and 100 percent of its water.

Packrats are a staple of numerous desert predators—foxes, coyotes, bobcats, snakes, and the like. These predators owe much to the cacti which are so adept at supporting so many of the desert's small creatures.

Another animal greatly dependent on prickly pears and chollas is the javelina. This small wild pig, also called a peccary, relies heavily on cactus pads and fruits for food and moisture. To come on a noisy band of feeding javelinas is quite a sight. Like domestic pigs, they are great rooters. They use their sturdy hooves and their long leathery snouts to dig up roots and yank out vegetation. In a very short time they can leave a whole area practically void of all living matter. The beasts are completely undisturbed by sharp spines. Even barrel cacti are not immune to them.

Close to fifty kinds of animals rely, to some extent, on prickly pears for food. Rodents are particularly partial to them. The Harris ground squirrel gets two-thirds of its nourishment from prickly pear seeds. Other animals have a more casual dependence on them. Almost all the desert animals, vegetarian or carnivore, enjoy cactus fruit. And some of the larger animals—pronghorns, deer, and cattle—will eat cactus stems in times of need.

During one visit to Saguaro National Monument I came upon a creature I never expected to see in the wild. It found yet another use for these plants.

Gila monster

It was about 9:30 or 10:00 in the morning. I had been walking about since daybreak taking pictures, studying the cacti, and looking for animals when I saw something black moving slowly across a paved road ahead of me. As I got closer I realized that it was a gila monster, one of the desert's most notorious creatures.

The gila monster is our largest lizard and our only poisonous one. Naturally my pulse quickened when I recognized what it was. I moved forward, hardly breathing, not wanting to frighten or agitate it. Its thick eighteen-inch body was covered with black and peach-colored scales arranged in a lovely mosaic pattern. The gila monster quickened its pace as I moved closer, but in no sense was it in a real hurry. It headed slowly but without hesitation for the shadows of a clump of prickly pear maybe ten feet away. Once under the protective covering of the cacti, the gila monster turned toward me, flicking its black tongue all the while. After the initial shock of seeing the animal face to face, I realized I was in no danger as long as I remained a few feet away. The monster had no inclination to attack. Although it could deliver a nasty venomous bite if it wished, it actually was a retiring fellow as others have claimed. We stood face to face for a few moments. I shifted my weight and it turned, retreating further into the shade of the prickly pear. The prickly pear served it well, discouraging a snoop like me from bothering it further. How many creatures must owe their well-being to the protective covering of these odd plants!

Javelinas feeding

Tit for Tat   As you can see, cacti in many ways serve the animals that share their communities. Their good deeds do not go unrewarded. For in the desert, animals serve the cacti they depend on in various ways.

Many birds are insect vigilantes. They help rid cacti of harmful boring insects. The gilas and gildeds perform this service for the saguaros. One of their favorite foods is a moth larva which bores into the saguaros and brings a disease which is dangerous to the plants. When the woodpeckers are not digging a nest, or sipping nectar, they may be tunneling after these or other bark-boring insects.

Perhaps the greatest service comes from the pollinators. A number of winged creatures—birds, moths, bees, and bats—carry pollen from one blossom to another as they feed on cacti blossoms. This helps to pollinate the cactus flowers and thus fertilize the ovules. Saguaro pollen is too heavy to be carried by wind. Without the doves, the long-nosed bats, and the bees which pollinate them, the plants could not produce seeds and they would soon die out.

A deer who nibbles a cactus fruit and then passes the seeds through its droppings is helping to spread seeds. A ground squirrel who picks up seeds to take back to its nests and drops some along the way is spreading seeds. So is an animal that picks up a cactus fruit, partially eats it, and leaves the remainder far from the base of the fruiting plant. These animals are not intending to do so, but they are sowing seeds, spreading them about where other plants are not claiming the nutrients and moisture from the soil.

Animals are helping plant life when they spread seeds. But of course they are destroying it when they are eating seeds. A balance is necessary. Natural predators are necessary to that balance.

In the 1930s cattle ranchers in the Sonoran Desert banded together to eliminate the coyote. They were quite effective in doing so. In a few years the desert's rodent population doubled and tripled. Today in some parts of the desert very few new saguaros are growing up. It appears that rodents ate most of the saguaro seeds and seedlings produced in that time. Naturalists worry that the effects of the coyote control program may be very long-lasting.

Some cacti reproduce by vegetative means. Jumping chollas do not produce many seeds. Their main means of reproducing is through the rooting of fallen joints. (See p. 12.) Animals help in this vegetative propagation. Each time an animal bumps into a cholla and gets a spiny joint stuck in its fur, it carries the stem to a new spot. Out of the range of the parent plant's vast root system, the stem has a better chance of rooting and developing into a new plant. As you can guess, the packrats are helping in this process when they pick up cholla joints and take them back to their nests. Some are certain to take root and eventually become new plants.

You know the importance of the earthworm to a garden. It helps to aerate the soil by tunneling through it. In the desert this work is done by the host of little creatures that burrow into the soil in retreat from the scorching heat. As you walk across any expanse of the desert floor, you come across hole after hole. Most animals build more than one tunnel into the soil. Kangaroo rats, ground squirrels, and other creatures make elaborate networks of tunnels and chambers. All the digging helps to loosen the soil and aids in getting air into it. This is a boon to the cacti and other desert plants that must send their tender roots into the soil to collect water and nutrients.

Living side by side with the cacti throughout their range are many interesting succulents, trees, shrubs, bushes, wildflowers, and herbs. All have solved the problem of surviving in the desert. And all are valuable to the animals in the community. They are in many ways important to each other and to the cacti, too.

Any plant with a vast network of roots helps to hold soil and secure it from wind and flood. Cacti help in this work and their neighbors do, too. The creosote bush (see pp. 4–5), which is common throughout the Sonoran, Chihuahuan, and Mojave deserts, is particularly valuable as a soil stabilizer. Naturally, without soil cacti and other plants could not get the nutrients they need to survive.

Creosote bushes and a few other plants are of special importance to the saguaros. Like most cacti, a saguaro is slow growing. Its infancy is very long. At two years old a saguaro is not even an inch tall. At age nine or ten it is only six inches tall. It will be fifteen before it reaches one foot; twenty-five before it reaches three feet. Until it is several feet tall, the saguaro needs shade. Creosote bushes or desert trees often supply this shade for infant and adolescent saguaros. The saguaro may spend thirty to fifty years in the protection of the "nurse" plant. Finally the nurse dies and the saguaro grows up and dominates the spot first claimed by its nurse.

SAGUARO GROWTH

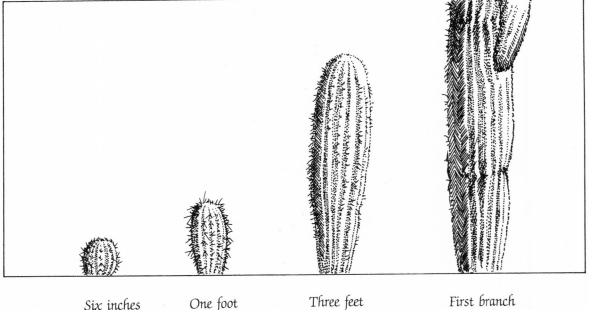

| Six inches
at 10 years | One foot
at 15 years | Three feet
at 25 years | First branch
at 65 years |

In Death They Also Serve   Just as the fallen leaves of a tree or its rotting trunk help to enrich the soil in a forest, so the withered stems of a dying cactus help to enrich the desert soil. Though desert soil is not as rich in decayed plant and animal material as is that of a forest, each dead plant and animal does contribute.

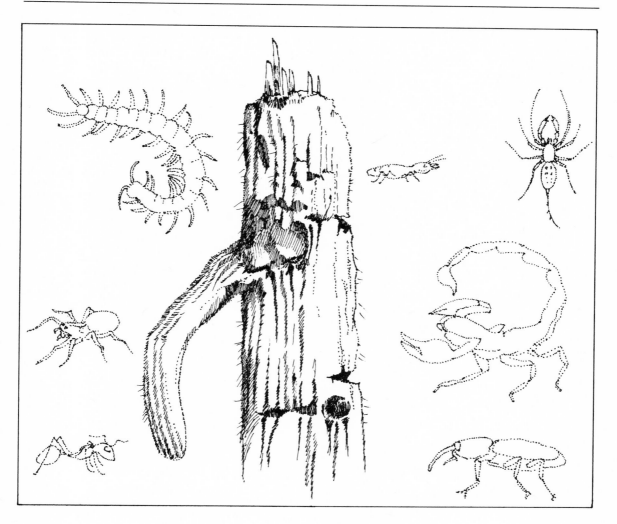

It is a common sight throughout the desert to come upon the dying hulks and dead skeletons of the larger cacti, saguaros, and chollas in particular. Long after their succulent tissue has been consumed or has disintegrated, the woodlike skeletons remain on the desert floor. These serve as a haven to certain desert animals, just as a dying oak is a haven in its habitat. An old saguaro skeleton is a perfect place for termites, spiders, ants, scorpions, and occasionally a shy gila monster.

Life around a dead saguaro

CHAPTER FOUR

Spiny, and What Else?

Hamatocactus uncinatus

Most people can tell that saguaros and prickly pears are cacti. Their thick, spiny stems are easy to recognize. But not all cacti are so easily recognized and a number of other spiny plants are often confused with cacti.

THE DISTINGUISHING FEATURES

How can you tell that a plant is a cactus? Basically cacti have five distinguishing features.

Areoles

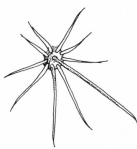

Areole

Many plants are covered with spines. Each has its own particular kind of spininess. Here are some examples:

Examine a rose and you will see that its prickles grow singly along its stems. Each is a separate unit attached directly to the stem and looking almost glued on. A rose's prickles develop from the superficial tissue of the stem and can be knocked off easily.

The agave, or century plant, found throughout the Southwest also comes armored with single prickles. Instead of being sprinkled randomly and superficially along a stem, however, the prickles of the agave are set in rows along the edges of its leaves. They look like so many rows of teeth.

An ocotillo's thorns are the hardened remainders of leaf stalks which have dropped their leaves. They grow up and down the woody, whip-shape branches of the plant looking like the spikes on a medieval weapon.

The long straight spikes of a mesquite tree come set in pairs along its branches, together with pairs of leaflets.

A cactus's spines differ from those of other spiny plants, and they are set upon the plant differently. In general they grow in clusters. Three, four, even dozens grow from one spot. But more importantly, they grow out of special budding organs called *areoles*.

The word *areole* comes from Latin and means "little area." To the naked eye these areoles look like fuzzy dots, something like the raised dots on dotted swiss, a fabric often used for curtains and pinafores. Under a magnifying glass these areoles look like little balls of cotton. All new growth—new branches, spines, flowers, fruits, leaves—develops from these cottony spine cushions.

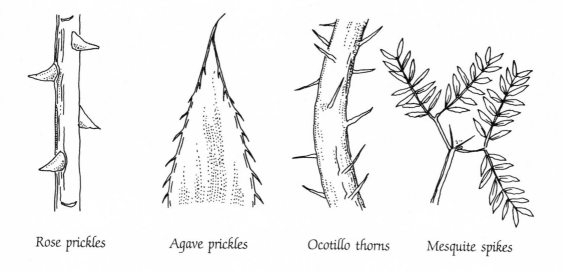

Rose prickles   Agave prickles   Ocotillo thorns   Mesquite spikes

No other plants in the plant kingdom have areoles. These special organs distinguish cacti from all other plants.

You will find these areoles arranged in spirals across the flat surfaces of prickly pears. On other cacti you may find them elevated on the edges of pleats, called ribs, or on tubercles. A *tubercle* is a warty projection or mound which gives a plant a bumpy appearance. In some cacti with flat narrow stems, areoles occur in notches along the stem's edge.

Succulent plants can be divided into two types. Those with thickened leaves such as century plants are called *leaf succulents*. Those with thick-

Leafless and Succulent

ened stems are called *stem succulents*. Cacti are stem succulents. We have already seen that most are leafless. There are only a few exceptions. Some of the prickly pears, for instance, produce leaves on new growth, but these tend to be small and insignificant and short lived. Generally they drop off as soon as the stems begin to mature. Only the pereskias and a few other ancient groups of cacti retain leaves throughout the life of the plant. As a general characteristic, cacti are said to be leafless plants.

Flowers of Distinction

You have already seen how beautiful are the flowers of the saguaro. Having flowers of great beauty is not unusual among the cacti. Cacti bear some of the most beautiful flowers in the plant kingdom. Some are so exquisite in form, so brilliant in color, and so lush in texture, that they are rivaled only by the most exotic rare flowers. Perhaps you are familiar with the tropical cacti called epiphyllums. These are grown by flower fanciers around the world.

Though we appreciate flowers for their beauty, they have a greater importance to the plant itself. The flower is an organ without which the plant could not produce the seeds it needs for reproduction. Flowers differ greatly from plant family to plant family and often are important in helping us to distinguish similar looking plants from each other.

Basically, there are four parts to a flower—petals, sepals, pistils, and stamens. Most people can readily identify a flower's petals. These are the showy inner leaves of the flower, often brightly colored. The sepals are the outer leaves of the flower. They surround the flower bud before the flower opens and are found beneath the petals after the flower has bloomed. Generally they are green. The pistil is the female or seed-producing organ, and the stamens are the male or pollen-producing organs. Pistils and stamens form the center, or inside, of most flowers. The stamens are often yellow tipped.

Not all flowers have all four parts. Those that do are called complete or perfect flowers.

Cactus flowers are complete, but not typical. Their petals and sepals

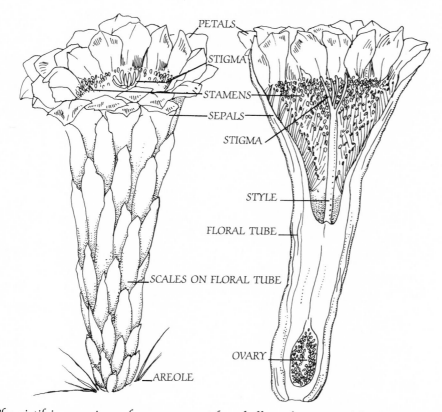

PETALS
STIGMA
STAMENS
SEPALS
STIGMA
STYLE
FLORAL TUBE
SCALES ON FLORAL TUBE
OVARY
AREOLE

The pistil is a syringe-shape organ with a bulbous bottom and long neck that branches at the top. The bulbous portion is the seed-producing ovary. It becomes the fruit. The neck is called the style; the branches, the stigma lobes. Pollen trapped by the stigmas sends down tubes through the style to the ovary below and fertilizes the ovules which become the plant's seeds.

STRUCTURE OF A FLOWER

In a simple complete flower the ovary and style form a compact pistil and are located above the petals and sepals. In a cactus flower the ovary is located below the petals and sepals sometimes way down at the base of a floral tube. The style however remains above the petals and sepals.

In some plant families flowers have more than one style. The cactus flower always has just one. Its stamens, however, are generally numerous, numbering over a thousand in some species. Each stamen consists of a stalk or filament which is topped by an anther composed of pollen sacs.

are not always easy to distinguish and their organs are arranged differently from those of other plants with complete flowers.

In most flowering plants, the ovary, which becomes the fruit, is located above the petals and sepals. In the cactus the ovary is located below the petals and sepals within a fleshy receptacle. In many cactus species this receptacle is long and tubelike, and then the ovary is found way down at the base of the tube. The tube or receptacle is covered by scalelike leaves. It may also have spines.

One-celled Fruits

Only flowering plants produce fruit. A fruit is nothing more than a flower ovary which has matured. As the flower petals wither and fall off, the ovary within the pistil grows and changes texture and its ovules mature into seeds.

The cactus produces a kind of fruit called a one-celled berry. It has no special chambers or divisions in which the seeds grow. Rather, its seeds are scattered throughout the pulp as are the seeds in a watermelon.

All cacti bear fruit. Many are quite fleshy and juicy; others may be hard, leathery, dry, or woody.

SOME CACTUS FRUITS

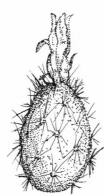

A HEDGEHOG   A PRICKLY PEAR   ANOTHER   A SAGUARO   CROSS-SECTION
                                            HEDGEHOG   OF A SAGUARO

Seedling cacti begin life looking like tiny kitten heads. The seed takes root, begins to sprout, and develops two embryo leaves called *cotyledons*, which resemble tiny ears. Between the two leaves a tuft of spines develops and becomes the cactus plant. Eventually the two embryo leaves drop or wither away.

Two Embryo Leaves

A cactus seedling showing cotyledons

PLANTS THAT CONFUSE

Once the distinguishing features of a cactus are learned, it becomes fairly easy to distinguish the typical cactus from other spiny plants of the desert. These other plants may be spiny or succulent or both, and they may be oddly shaped, but they really aren't much like cacti.

Look at the two drawings on pp. 52–53. The spine-tipped, tooth-edged agave on the left is often mistaken for a cactus. Notice how it differs from the cactus on the right. Not only are its spines simply jagged thorny ridges, they do not grow from areoles. Notice also that its blossom rises from a stalk at the center of the plant. A cactus flower grows from an areole located on a stem. The agave blossom is a torch-shape collection of many blossoms massed together. A typical cactus blossom is composed of one set of petals and sepals arising from a single floral tube or cup. Most are trumpet- or bell-shape.

Now look at the drawing on the right. This is an organ-pipe cactus. It is native to southern Arizona and Mexico and is the major attraction at the national monument which took its name. Notice how it differs from the agave. It is composed of several cylindrical, succulent, and spiny stems. Like a saguaro, its stems are ribbed or pleated. Along the tops of the ribs are the areoles from which the clusters of spines grow. The tubelike flowers also grow from these areoles toward the ends of the branches. The plant is leafless. It is not much like an agave at all.

There is a group of plants that you might come across in botanical gardens that can be mistaken for cacti, the euphorbias. Many of the plants in this group resemble cacti more closely than any other plant group. Like cacti, they are stem succulents and the shapes of some are

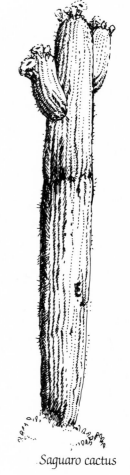

Saguaro cactus

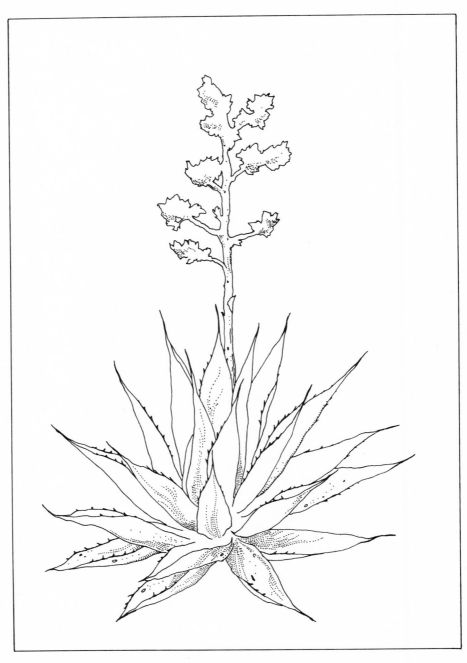

An agave

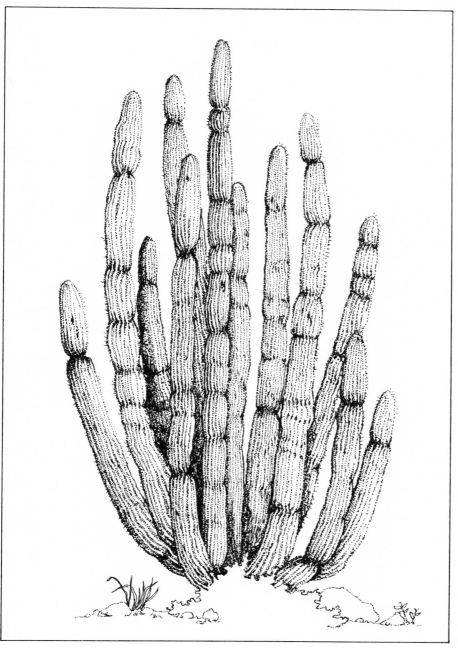

Organ-pipe cactus

very cactuslike. The euphorbias developed in the Old World and most are native to it. While cacti were developing in response to the dry conditions of the New World, these Old World succulents developed in a similar fashion to withstand the rigors of life in the deserts of Africa, Arabia, Madagascar, and Sri Lanka.

Similar, but Varied

Cacti have been particularly successful in adapting to the climate of southern Arizona. Some forty or more species can be found growing in a 150-mile radius around Tucson. But as rich as the cactus life is there, it represents only a sampling of the many plants making up the cactus family.

It is not possible to give an exact count of the number of cactus species scattered across the Western Hemisphere. New species are discovered from time to time and the experts disagree on whether some plants are actually different species or just variations of the same plant. Some say there are eight hundred or more distinct species. Others put the number as high as three thousand. A species is a group of plants or animals with common characteristics. The members of a species can readily interbreed and reproduce.

Although all cacti share certain characteristics, as a family of plants they show amazing variety. Not only do they vary in shape and size, but their spines, fruits, and flowers vary greatly as well.

Some Cactus Shapes and Ways of Growing

The shape of cactus stems varies from columnar as in a saguaro to globose as in a barrel cactus. (See p. 7.) There are also words to describe the shapes of cactus silhouettes and how they grow. A cactus may be branched or unbranched, jointed or unjointed. It may be prostrate or erect, creeping or pendent, vinelike or treelike, to name a few. These words describe shapes and ways of growing. Some examples may be found on pp. 18–19.

An organ-pipe is a columnar cactus. Its cylindrical branches are only occasionally jointed. A prickly pear is a flat-jointed plant which sometimes branches and sometimes does not. Some prickly pears are prostrate; their joints or stems grow along the ground. Others stand erect. A barrel cactus can be globose or cylindrical. It is not jointed and most often is not branched. Most barrel cacti consist of a single stem, though some may have several heads (individual stems).

A euphorbia

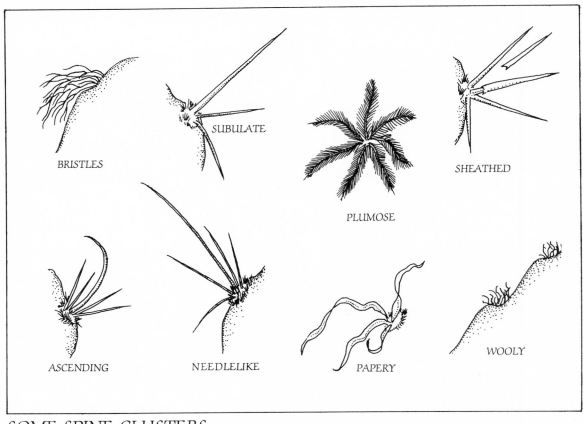

BRISTLES

SUBULATE

PLUMOSE

SHEATHED

ASCENDING

NEEDLELIKE

PAPERY

WOOLY

SOME SPINE CLUSTERS

Types of Spines

Most cacti are spiny, at least when they are young. Some have only one type of spine. Others may have two or three types. The variations are endless.

Cactus spines can be quite decorative. Many plant hobbyists are as attracted to a plant for its spines as they are for its flowers. It is helpful to become familiar with the names of the various types of spines. When cacti are described by scientists, these terms are used.

In plants with more than one type of spine, often a central spine is surrounded by a group of smaller spines called the radial spines.

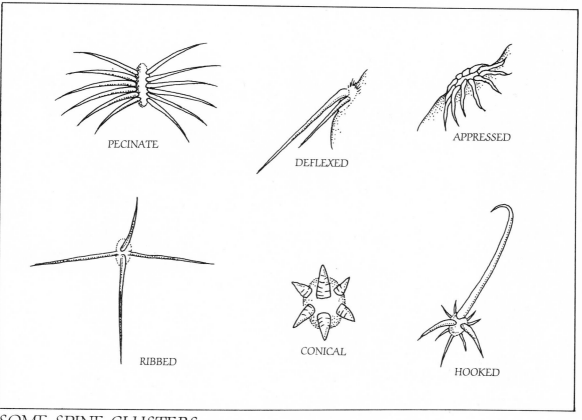

SOME SPINE CLUSTERS

The prickly pear group of cacti have tufts of tiny barbed bristles called glochids either in addition to regular spines or in place of them. To the naked eye the glochids might look like the soft tip of a fine brush, but touch them and you will find that they are fiercely tenacious. The minute barbs will lodge in your finger and be difficult to remove.

Cactus spines range in color as well as shape. The most common color is probably brown or tan, but they also come in white, yellow, various shades of red and orange, gray, and black. Some are tipped with a bright color as if they had been dipped in paint.

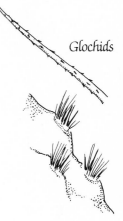

Glochids

WAYS OF FLOWERING

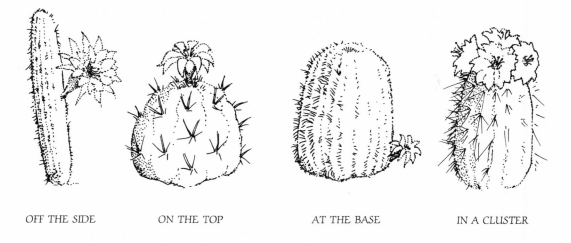

OFF THE SIDE   ON THE TOP   AT THE BASE   IN A CLUSTER

Flower Variations

Though all cactus flowers are complete, they vary in shape and color. Petals vary in size and shape as well, though in most cacti they are numerous and quite showy.

In identifying cacti it is important to determine from what point on the stem its flowers develop. In most the flowers grow from areoles, but this may be off the side of a stem, on the top, or even at the base. The cactus may produce only one or two flowers per stem, or as in some species, a number of flowers develop in a cluster off a stem or in a ring around the stem at top or bottom. Except in the pereskias, each flower comes from a separate areole. In most it is borne on a tube.

Fruit Variations

Fruits vary in cacti as greatly as flowers do. They may be even skinned or tubercled. Some are spiny. Most at least have leaf scales to begin with. They vary from the size of a pea to a grapefruit. In some the pulp is meaty, juicy, sweet, and delicious. In others it is dry and hard and inedible. Seeds vary greatly as well.

WAYS OF FLOWERING

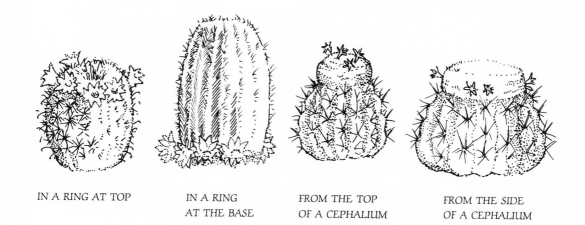

IN A RING AT TOP   IN A RING AT THE BASE   FROM THE TOP OF A CEPHALIUM   FROM THE SIDE OF A CEPHALIUM

Suppose you found an unfamiliar cactus. How would you find out its name?

The best place to look would be in a handbook or field guide. In trying to fit a plant to a description, be warned about this: A young plant will not necessarily have the characteristics of an adult plant. To identify a plant properly, often you must be able to examine a mature specimen in the field. And you may need to see all its parts—its stems, flowers, fruits, roots, and seeds—before determining what species it is. Even experts have trouble distinguishing a particular species. The hours spent in identifying an unfamiliar plant can be very rewarding when met with success, but fruitless research can be very frustrating.

To make your task easier, a list of helpful books appears in the bibliography at the back of this book, as does an explanation of Latin classifications. Other guides may be obtained in local areas, and pp. 62–89 will introduce you to a few of our common or most popular cactus species.

Identifying Cacti

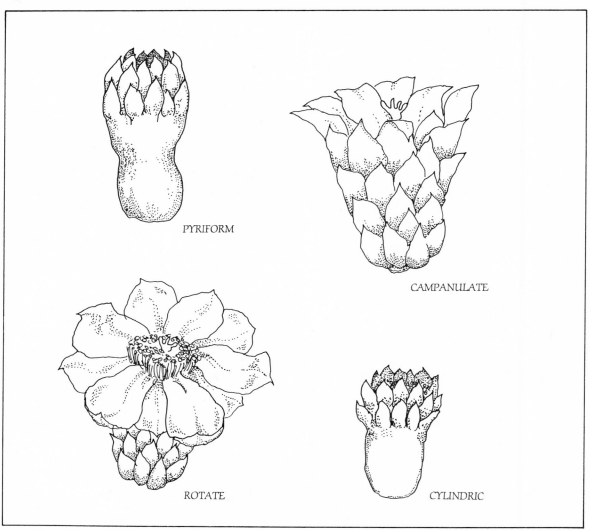

PYRIFORM

CAMPANULATE

ROTATE

CYLINDRIC

SOME FLOWER SHAPES

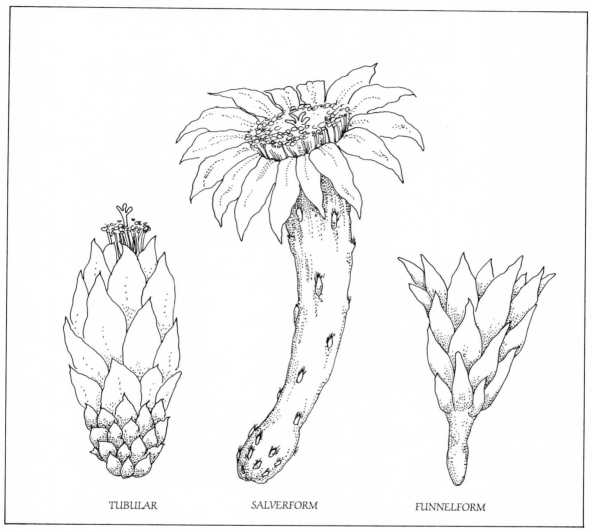

TUBULAR   SALVERFORM   FUNNELFORM

SOME FLOWER SHAPES

Cactus common names can be fascinating and fun. Sometimes they describe the color of the plant or the shape of its flower or fruit. Often the name suggests a thing or animal the plant resembles.

The prickly pears are particularly rich in names. There are bunny ears prickly pears, cow's tongue prickly pears, hedgehog prickly pears, and pancake prickly pears. A favorite is the *beaver's tail prickly pear,* which got its name for the obvious reason that its flat, bluish-green stems resemble beavers' tails. These stems are covered with minute hairs, and velvety-looking glochids fill their areoles. Don't be fooled, though. Those innocent-looking glochids are barbed and troublesome—not furry.

Beaver's tails are native throughout much of Arizona, Utah, Nevada, New Mexico, and California, although several varieties seem to be disappearing. They are low-growing, clump-forming plants with six- to twelve-inch stems. These stems may be eaten as a vegetable. The plant is used in gardens, especially in the Southwest.

FLOWER: Large and showy; purple to pink or yellow to white.
FRUIT: Green when young; tan or gray when mature; spineless and dry.
SPINE CLUSTER: No spines; glochids brown or reddish-brown, about one-eighth inch long.

WORRISOME BEAVER'S TAILS

Opuntia basilaris

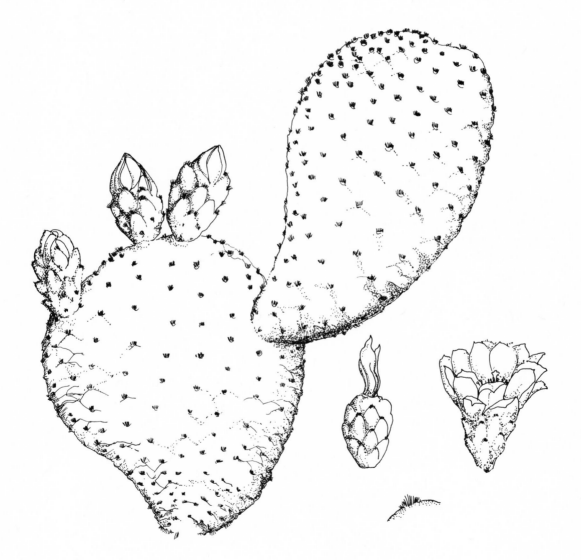

Easterner's
Prickly Pear

Here is a cactus Easterners can find growing in their own backyards. It grows in sandy and rocky places from Cape Cod to North Carolina and in mountain areas from Alabama to Canada and westward to Northern Illinois, eastern Missouri, and Tennessee. Most likely the Pilgrims became acquainted with it as they explored Cape Cod.

Low and spreading and often spineless, this dark green prickly pear is easily overlooked throughout most of the year. Come summer, though, and its cheery yellow flowers draw attention to the plant.

I first came upon the *eastern prickly pear* on a sandy, rutty road on the North Carolina coast. Never having seen a cactus outside the Southwest, I was a bit surprised. Like many people, I had thought that cacti were exclusively desert plants. I had assumed, quite wrongly, that someone had planted the low-growing cactus.

FLOWER: Small; yellow.
FRUIT: Spineless; red; juicy and edible.
SPINE CLUSTER: No spines, or perhaps just one stout white, gray, or
     yellowish one; glochids yellowish- or greenish-brown.

EASTERNER'S PRICKLY PEAR

Opuntia humifusa (also Opuntia compressa)

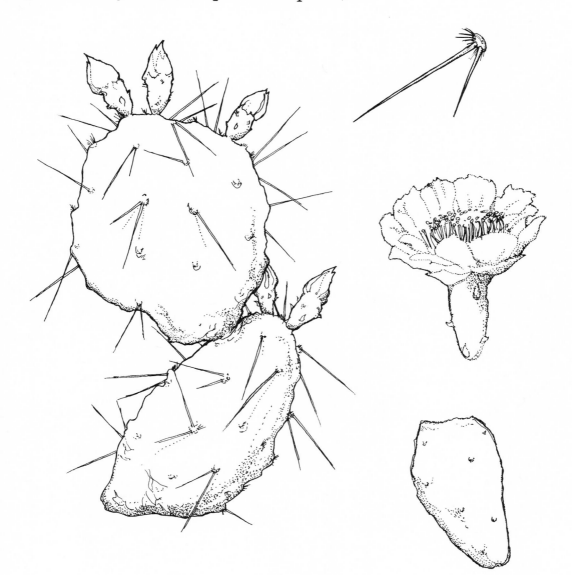

Purple-fruited Prickly Pears

If you were to take a trip through the Southwest, you would undoubtedly come across one or two of the four varieties of *purple-fruited prickly pears*. These plants grow in Arizona, Utah, Colorado, New Mexico, Texas, and Mexico. They are quite common in some areas and to many Southwesterners they have no name other than simply "prickly pears."

The species varies greatly. It may be low and sprawling or erect and bushlike. The plant produces a mass of joints which in an older plant can create a clump twenty feet across. Eight-foot clumps are more typical, however. Its joints are bluish-green, though in winter they may be bordered or streaked with red. Joints range from four to six inches on some plants and from ten to sixteen inches on others.

Sweet and juicy, the fruits of these prickly pears make excellent jelly, syrup, and candy. They can be good thirst quenchers as well. Rodents, deer, javelina, and cattle are fond of the fruit.

One variety of this cactus, *Engelmann's prickly pear,* is the largest and best known of the Southwestern prickly pears. Some botanists call it *Opuntia engelmannii.* According to others its scientific name is *Opuntia phaeacantha,* variety *discata.*

Many plants are named after the person who discovered or first described it. Engelmann's was named after Dr. George Engelmann, a nineteenth-century doctor of medicine who studied cacti in his spare time. He was the first great student of American cacti and contributed greatly to our understanding of the plants. His headquarters were at the Missouri Botanical Garden in St. Louis.

The areoles on all the purple-fruited prickly pears are few and rather far apart, each sporting only a few spines. In most varieties the spines are more numerous in the upper areoles. This is not true of Engelmann's. Spines occur uniformly over most of the plant.

FLOWER: Yellow in most; in some red at the base.
FRUIT: Smooth; purple to deep red; generally sweet and juicy.
SPINE CLUSTER: Highly variable; in variety *phaeacantha,* three to five or sometimes nine long brown spines, straight or deflexed; in the variety called Engelmann's, relatively short and white.

PURPLE-FRUITED PRICKLY PEARS

Opuntia phaeacantha (also Opuntia engelmannii)

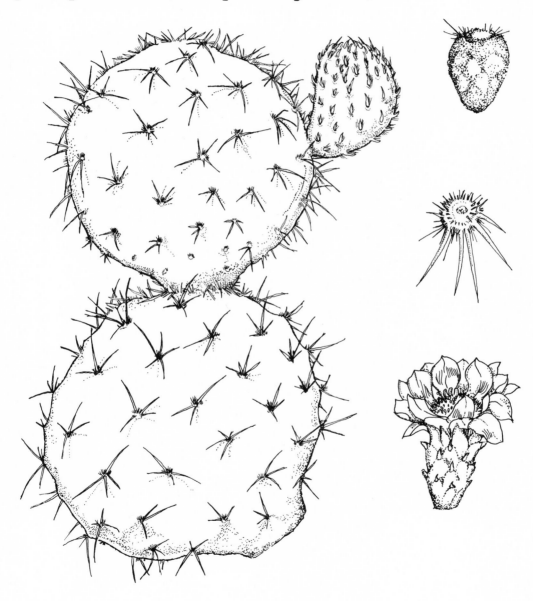

**Touch-me-not
Teddy Bear**

At a distance the *teddy bear* looks quite huggable. Covered with straw-colored sheaths, its numerous spines give this cactus a glistening, furry, teddy-bear appearance. Up close, though, beware. The teddy bear becomes ferocious. The sheath-covered spines are barbed and dangerous and hard to remove.

The teddy bear is one of two chollas often called a "jumping cholla." Its many branches are very brittle. At the slightest touch they snap off and cling to the unwitting person or creature who chances to come too close. So suddenly does this happen that the branches seem to jump right off the plant.

Although harpooning unsuspecting victims seems like a needlessly ugly trait, it is important to the plant's survival. The plant relies on the broken joints to perpetuate the species. When the joints fall to the ground, they take root. Eventually they become new plants.

The teddy bear cholla is a fairly small, shrub-size cactus, generally growing to about four feet. As the plant matures, the branches at the bottom of its trunk die and turn black. The plant grows in Nevada, California, and Arizona and often forms thick stands. A nice stand is protected in Joshua Tree National monument in California.

FLOWER: Small; pale green, yellow, or white.
FRUIT: Small; usually spineless; contain only a few seeds.
SPINE CLUSTER: Six to ten pinkish-tan or reddish-brown strong barbed and sheathed spines which spread in all directions. Yellowish glohids.

TOUCH-ME-NOT TEDDY BEAR

Opuntia bigelovii

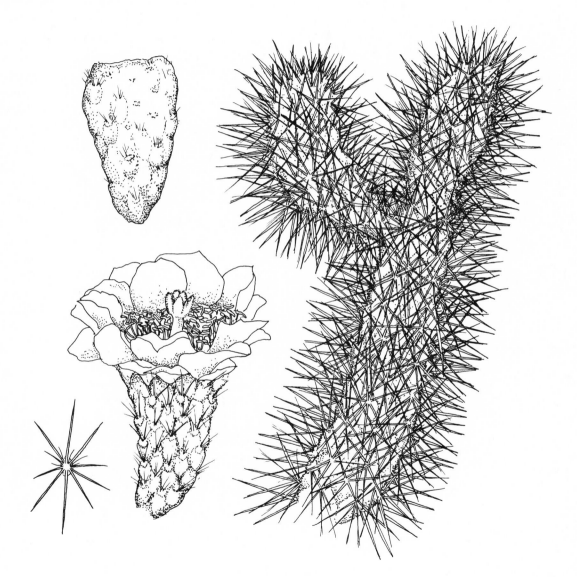

Chains of Fruit

Here is another jumping cholla with sheathed spines and that nasty trait of clinging to anyone who chances to touch it. If you can overlook this trait and free your imagination, you might see the *chain fruit cholla* in a different light. It is a most striking, treelike cactus whose many spiny branches hang heavy with long chains of small green fruits. Often a single chain may hold twelve or more links.

When heavily laden, the plant looks almost biblical. You can imagine that it might have held a prominent spot in the Garden of Eden where Adam and Eve first walked. It seems that you could pluck a fruit from one of the cholla's chains and another would miraculously pop up in its place.

This does happen, in a sense. But the process takes a year. Each year the plant produces small flowers and each year these wither to be replaced by tiny green fruits. The fruits do not ripen and they do not fall off the plant. Next year's blossoms and fruit develop out of last year's fruit. Eventually a long chain of fruit is formed. Unfortunately, the fruits are not edible. What a shame that such a bountiful plant is only a teaser!

These chollas, which get to be about twelve feet tall, can form impenetrable forests. Such forests used to be fairly common in southern Arizona where the chain fruit chollas grow, but most have been bulldozed down. Southern Arizona is rapidly growing and the old cactus habitats are being used for homes and businesses.

FLOWER: Small; rose or lavender.

FRUIT: Small; green; spineless; grow in chains.

SPINE CLUSTER: Six to twelve, sometimes less, straight needlelike or awl-shape barbed and sheathed spines which spread in all directions; glochids yellowish.

CHAINS OF FRUIT

Opuntia fulgida

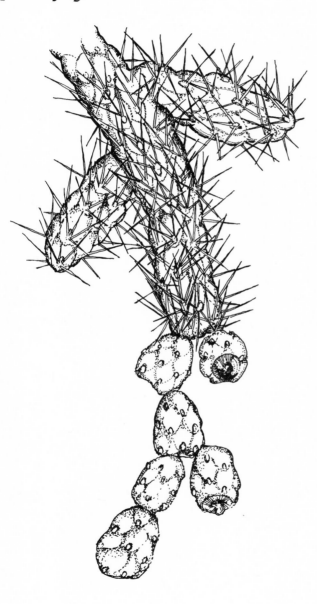

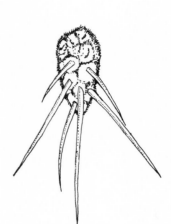

Fragrant
Night-bloomer

The exotic perfume of the desert *night-blooming cereus* is so powerful and pungent that it can be detected a quarter of a mile away. Unfortunately its powerful sweet perfume was not meant for human nostrils, and the beauty of its large flowers was not meant for human eyes. The plant, as its name suggests, blooms at night. The purpose: to attract night-flying animals.

Though its blossoms are among the most beautiful in the cactus family, the night-blooming cereus itself is not at all attractive. It is a scraggly, dead-looking collection of narrow ribbed stems which hide under shrubs and trees and for the most part go unnoticed. If one were to look very hard, this plant could be found in Texas, New Mexico, Arizona, and Mexico.

You may wonder how such a straggly, insignificant plant produces some of the most beautiful flowers in the world. The secret lies underground. The plant has an enormous tuberous root. The root looks like a giant sweet potato or turnip. In some a root may weigh sixty pounds. During drought, the plant lives off the water that is stored in the succulent tissue inside the root, so that even in the driest years, flowers can be produced.

FLOWER: Large and showy; white or lavender; extremely long floral tube.

FRUIT: Spiny; red; sweet and juicy.

SPINE CLUSTER: Eleven to thirteen short, needlelike spines lying almost parallel to the surface of the stem; some dark, some white.

FRAGRANT NIGHT BLOOMER

Cereus greggii (also Peniocereus greggii)

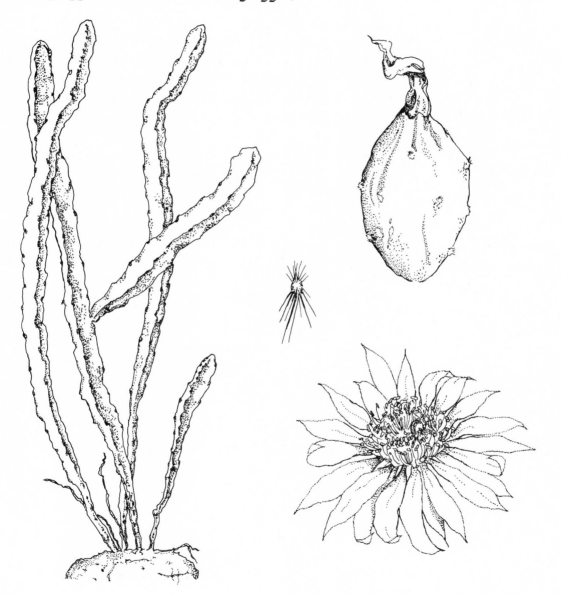

*Strawberries
in a Hedgehog*

A hedgehog is an Old World porcupine. As you can guess, most hedgehog cacti are fairly spiny. The Engelmann's, or strawberry, hedgehog has so many spines that its short, cylindrical stems are practically hidden.

This plant is the most common of the hedgehog cacti and one of the prominent plants of the Sonoran and Mojave (California) deserts, though a number of its variations are threatened or endangered. It also can be found in the Great Basin Desert of Nevada and Utah. As are most of the hedgehogs, it is a clustering plant, forming clumps of ribbed stems up to two or three feet in diameter. Each stem is from eight to twelve inches tall. Its sweet red fruit, which resemble strawberries, are prized by desert animals and were considered a delicacy by the Indians of the Southwest.

FLOWER: Showy; pink, rose, or purple.
FRUIT: Small; red; sweet and juicy.
SPINE CLUSTER: Ten to eighteen spines of various lengths; principal central ones long, declined and flattened, curved, straight, or twisted; radials spreading close to stem, straight, broad, and needlelike.

STRAWBERRIES IN A HEDGEHOG

Echinocereus engelmannii

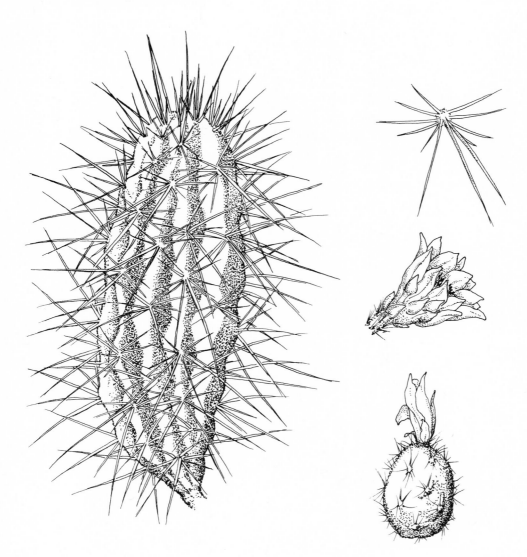

Lace Cactus

The *lace cactus*, a well-known plant, is favored by collectors not merely because of its large, colorful flowers but also for its decorative spines, which create a crocheted look. In the past the plant was widespread and fairly abundant throughout Oklahoma and Texas and occurred in Colorado, New Mexico, and Mexico as well. Now, however, it is disappearing throughout much of its range and certain varieties are endangered.

The plant may have one stem or a cluster of four- to twelve-inch upright, cylindrical stems. These have tubercled ribs.

FLOWER: Showy; purple or rose; wooly at the base.
FRUIT: Spiny; dry.
SPINE CLUSTER: Twenty to thirty yellowish to white spines arranged in comblike pattern and lying flat against the stem (appressed).

LACE CACTUS

Echinocereus caespitosus (also Echinocereus reichenbachii)

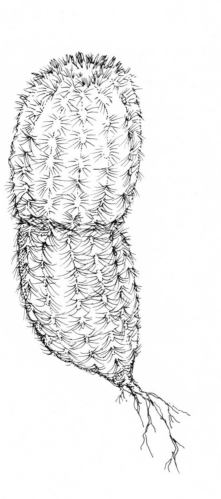

**Tubby
Touch-me-not**

People are affected by barrel cacti in different ways. To some they appear stately and venerable, worthy of respect. To others they are merely odd. To some they are feared and disliked. To me, there is something jolly about these tubby cacti, especially the round or globe-shape ones.

The *fishhook barrel cactus* is such a plant. It gets longish, up to eight to ten feet, in old age and is stately then. But as a young plant, it is stout, as wide as it is high, and rolypoly. It's hard for me to hold back a smile when I see one.

The fishhook barrel gets its name from the long hooked central spines that grow from each areole. The plant has fifteen to twenty ribs. Its flowers grow around the top of the plant in a circle. These are replaced by yellow fruits in winter which are a favorite food of desert animals.

The fishhook barrels are found in Texas, Arizona, New Mexico, and Mexico. It is easy to confuse them with another globose cactus, Coville's barrel (*Ferocactus covillei*), which also grows in Arizona and Mexico. Both have central hooked spines. In the Coville's barrel, however, the central hooked spine is accompanied by one kind of spine, not two.

FLOWER: Moderately showy; yellow-orange or red.
FRUIT: Scaly; yellow; fleshy.
SPINE CLUSTER: Four long, strongly cross-ribbed central spines, the
        longest hooked, surrounded by twelve to twenty slender gray-to-
        white irregularly curved or straight needlelike radial spines.

TUBBY TOUCH-ME-NOT

Ferocactus wislizenii (also Echinocactus wislizenii)

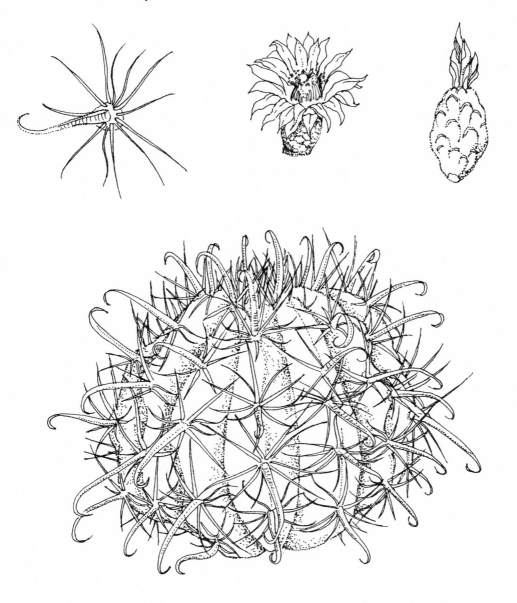

Many
Wooly Heads

You generally think of barrel cacti as solitary plants. But a number of them form huge clusters as they grow older.

The *wooly headed barrel* is solitary when young, but as it grows older, it begins adding heads (stems) until a mature one may have twenty or more. A clump of wooly heads two feet high and four feet in diameter is an impressive sight. Each head has thirteen to twenty-one ribs, is globose, and is densely covered with stout spines which originate from wooly areoles.

There are several varieties of the wooly headed barrel. It is one of the widest ranging of any cactus found in Texas. It is also found in Arizona, California, Nevada, Utah, and Mexico.

FLOWER: Yellow, sometimes tinged with pink; form a ring around the top of plant.

FRUIT: Dry; covered by a thick envelope of long white hairs.

SPINE CLUSTER: Four long, red, cross-ribbed central spines, each covered by an ash-colored coating, the lower one curved slightly downward; the others fairly straight. Six to eight similar, but smaller, radials, spreading irregularly or curving slightly.

MANY WOOLY HEADS

Echinocactus polycephalus

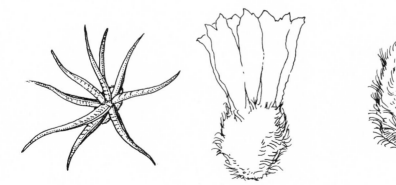

Horse Crippler   You know that any cactus with the name "horse crippler" has some devilish habits. The *horse crippler cactus* is the bane of many ranchers because of its habit of lying low, often under grass. It is a broad, low barrel cactus, rarely standing more than eight inches high. Its rigid spines can easily puncture the tender underside of a horse's or cow's hoof.

But while ranchers may dislike this cactus, collectors favor it. More hardy than most barrel cacti, it is easily adapted to cultivation. Its bell-shape flowers are beautiful and slightly fragrant.

Native throughout much of Texas, southwestern Oklahoma, New Mexico, and Mexico, it was at one time one of the widest ranging of the barrel cacti. Now, because ranchers have destroyed it and hobbyists have collected it, the plant is becoming rare.

FLOWER: Showy; pink.
FRUIT: Scaly and wooly; red; fleshy.
SPINE CLUSTER: Six to seven thick short, reddish, ringed radials which are reflexed backward; a single similar but stronger central spine, reflexed downward.

HORSE CRIPPLER

Echinocactus texensis (also Homalocephala texensis)

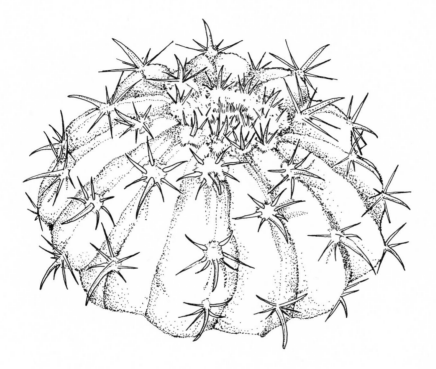

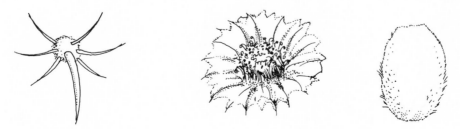

Living Rocks   Do you know what a horny toad looks like? Its horny body camouflages it and helps it hide among the rocks it lives among.

Living rock cacti have the same sort of camouflage. They are small, flat cacti that grow level with the ground. Their overlapping tubercles make them look like pieces of rock. As you can guess, these cacti are most often found on exposed rocky ridges. They are native to northern Mexico and southern Texas.

The plants do not have rigid spines. They don't need them because they are protected by a very firm, thick, warty skin. The tips of new growth are covered with long wool. The plants usually grow singly, but a few form clusters.

The living rock cacti are popular with hobbyists and are becoming rare from overcollecting. Don't confuse them with the group of succulents called "stone plants" or "living stones," the lithops. These are a noncactus group of plants from Africa.

FLOWER: Rose to purple; form a ring around the new growth of the plant.
FRUIT: Red; sweet and juicy.
SPINE CLUSTER: None; long wool on new growth.

LIVING ROCKS
Ariocarpus fissuratus

**Fishhook
Pincushions**

The mammillarias, or pincushion cacti, are fascinating. Most are only a few inches high or across, pincushion size, though some grow to a foot high and more. They come in a broad range of colors and those that cluster often form gorgeous geometric designs.

The mammillarias are basically North American plants. Some fourteen species are native to the United States.

The *fishhook pincushion* is common throughout its range which takes in west Texas, southern New Mexico, Arizona, and Mexico. With stems no more than six inches high, it is a dainty plant, single-stemmed when young and clustered when mature. As with all the mammillarias, it is tubercled. Areoles, one to a tubercle, are wooly when young and very spiny.

FLOWER: Rose to purple; form a ring around the new growth.
FRUIT: Red; sweet and juicy.
SPINE CLUSTER: Dark red central spine, or spines, the principal one hooked; eighteen to twenty-eight light tan-to-red long straight radial spines spreading parallel to stem.

FISHHOOK PINCUSHIONS

Mammillaria microcarpa

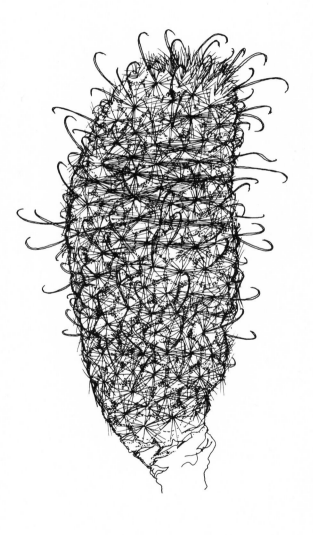

**Chilis
on a Pie Plate**

The *little chilis cactus* is one of the largest mammillarias found in the United States. Normally, this low, flat, single-stemmed plant is about five to eight inches in diameter—pie-plate size. Occasionally one will reach a diameter of twelve inches. Its habit of hugging the ground makes it difficult to see, however. It often goes unnoticed until it is in flower or in fruit. Then, these bright adornments form a ring around the top of the plant, the flowers looking like a wreath of asters; the fruit looking like an arrangement of small chilis. The plant ranges from Mexico across southwestern Texas, southern New Mexico, and into Arizona.

FLOWER: Small; pink, white, or cream.
FRUIT: Small; red; fleshy.
SPINE CLUSTER: Six to nine awl-shape, dark-tipped, straight or slightly curving radials spreading outward; straight, or slightly arched central spine.

CHILIS ON A PIE PLATE

Mammillaria gummifera variety meiacantha (also Mammillaria meiacantha)

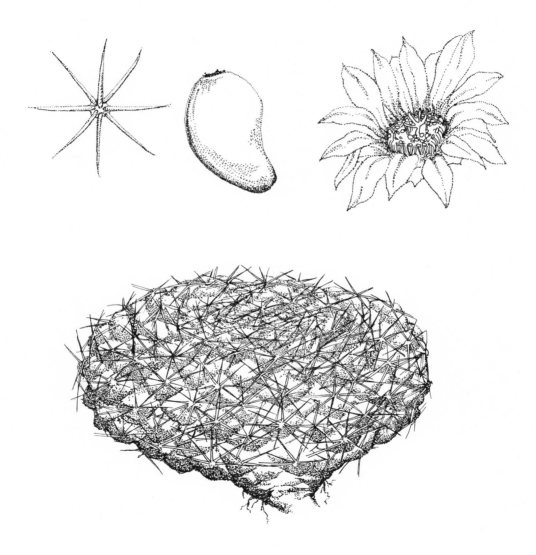

CHAPTER FIVE

Cactus Anyone? So Many Uses

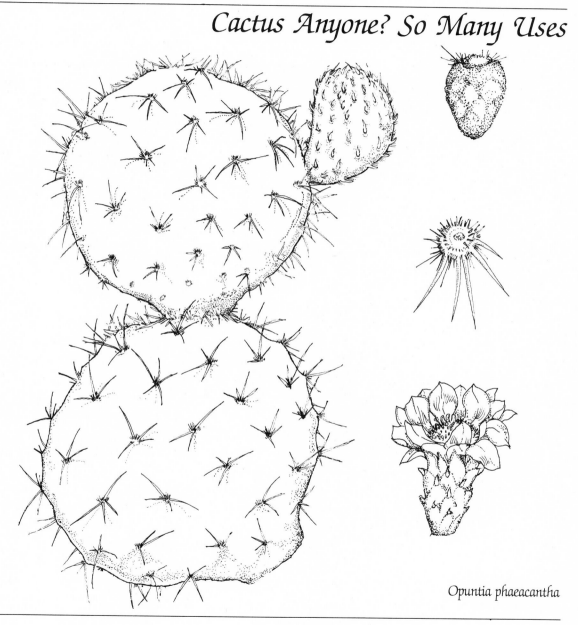

Opuntia phaeacantha

This scene has been dramatized over and over in the comics: The hero has been staggering across the desert in search of water. He is so weak he can hardly stand up. He stumbles over rocks, crashes into sticky bushes, sinks in deep sand. Finally, in the distance, he sees his salvation, a large barrel cactus which rises up from the desert like some miraculous root beer stand. One drink and he will be saved.

Such dramas are, of course, wild stretches of the truth. It is an exaggeration to think that a barrel cactus stands as a living water bucket in the middle of the desert. The plant is filled with a moist pulp, not standing water. To get at the moisture, one would have to squeeze, pound, or chew this pulp, and the taste would be bitter, perhaps even toxic. It could make you nauseous.

Nonetheless, barrel cacti have been known to quench the thirst of desert travelers. And cacti as a whole have been of great importance to people in other ways over the centuries.

In Mexico, Honduras, and the Canary Islands an important dye, called cochineal, is derived from a scalelike insect which lives on certain prickly pears. Large fields of the plants are cultivated to support the insects which are brushed off from time to time, dried, and ground to produce red, purple, and orange dyes.

The Papago Indians of the Sonoran Desert relied greatly on the saguaro cactus. They gathered its fruit, eating some raw and boiling the remainder into syrups, jellies, and jams. They ground its seeds into meal. And they used its woody interior ribs for building houses and making tools, carriers, and other useful objects. Even the saguaro spines were used—for needles and awls.

So important was the plant to these people that its blossoming time marked the beginning of their new year. Known as the Saguaro Harvest Moon, it was a time for joyous celebration. To welcome in the New Year, the Papagos made a sweet wine from the saguaro fruit.

Saguaro fruits are a good source of natural sugar and contain significant amounts of protein, fat, and Vitamin C. The early Spanish priests reported that the Papagos gained weight noticeably after gorging on saguaro fruits during their New Year's festivities.

Other cacti have been just as important to other ancient Indians throughout the Western Hemisphere. The fruits, stems, roots, buds, and leaves of many cacti are highly nutritious. The seeds, too, can be valuable and were collected by the ancients and ground into meal, pulverized for their oil, or roasted to be eaten as snacks. Cacti are portrayed among the ancient stone carvings of Mexico, showing their importance among the advanced civilizations there, and cacti loom large in the legends of Central America as far back as we know.

The ancients discovered a number of medicinal uses for cacti. Cactus pulp was used for salves and poultices to heal wounds and deaden pain. Other cacti were boiled for tea. The fuzzy spines of some were rubbed into moles and warts to remove them.

The woody skeletons of many of the large cacti had numerous uses. They were used for firewood as well as in the construction of houses, fences, and useful objects.

Today, cacti are used still in many of the ancient ways. The woody ribs are still used for firewood, for making fences and walls, and the like. A number of cacti are used as hedges and hedgerows. Can you think of any plant more likely to keep out unwanted persons than a row of tall prickly pears?

In this country cacti are used for cattle feed when forage is scarce and the hole-riddled skeletons of chollas are used in making a number of Southwestern craft items—trays, lamp bases, ornaments, picture frames. And, of course, many cacti are used in gardens.

Today, Indians still use cacti for medicinal reasons. Some are boiled and used as healing teas. Others are popular for killing pain and promoting healing. Peyote, a powerful narcotic which comes from a species of *Lophophora,* was used by ancient Mexicans to kill pain and cure illnesses and in some areas is still used. It is also used by some American Indians in religious services. Science may find other uses for this drug in the future.

Cactus fruits and stems are still eaten in many places. In Sicily prickly pears have been naturalized and their fruit has become a notable part of Italian cooking. In Spain, too, you can see prickly pears in many yards. And, of course, the fruit of prickly pears and other cacti can be had in many parts of Central and South America. Prickly pear fruits are popular in this country among Italian and Hispanic people. Many families plant prickly pears right outside the kitchen door.

The days when you could go out into our Southwestern deserts and harvest cacti as the Indians did are gone. In several states it is against the law to pick cacti except on your own land. And this is true on most federal lands as well. But cactus fruits and stems can be obtained here. A small cactus industry exists in California, which produces cactus fruits, tunas, and prickly pear stems, called *nopales* or *nopalitos*. These are grown on farms in several parts of the state.

The cacti grown in these orchards are domesticated prickly pears from Mexico, *Opuntia ficus-indica,* the Indian fig, or one of several hybrid cacti developed by the great plant scientist Luther Burbank.

In the spring the plants produce new stems. These new shoots are harvested and sold fresh or canned.

The fruits begin appearing in summer. As they ripen they are harvested. Some are sold fresh. Others are processed into jellies, preserves, and candies.

CACTUS COOKERY

It is fun to experiment with cactus stems and fruits. They add a touch of authenticity to Southwestern cooking. You can use fresh *nopalitos* and prickly pear fruits, tunas, in season. When fresh cactus products are not available, you can substitute canned products. You can get cactus jellies, preserves, candies, and canned *nopalitos* in the Mexican food section of many markets or at specialty food shops. Two types of *nopalitos* are sold: *Nopalitos Tiernos* are cactus stems which have been cooked tender. They come diced in sixteen- or twenty-two-ounce jars. *Nopalitos en Escabeche,* or marinated cactus, are pickled cactus stems. They also come diced in jars.

I shall never forget one cold February evening in Connecticut when I served a cactus dinner to friends. I had brought back some jars of *nopalitos* and other cactus products from the Southwest. It seemed like a good time to have a warming cactus feast. Except for a chicken tamale pie and the bread, every dish contained cactus stems or fruit.

First we had two dips, one a blend of *nopalitos* and cottage cheese and the other a mixture of guacamole and *nopalitos*. We had these with tortilla chips and celery sticks. I also passed around some crackers topped with cream cheese, a piece of cactus stem, and a spicy hot pepper jelly. The main course was the chicken tamale pie. With this we had a three bean and *nopalitos* salad, bread, and butter. For desert we had a lovely prickly pear jelly roll followed by coffee and prickly pear candy. What a meal! The tangy cacti flavors mingled with the hot chili peppers to bring a glow of the warm Southwest to our cold New England dining room.

Some of the recipes I used that night are in this chapter, along with a number of others. If you want to cook with cacti, don't be afraid to create your own recipes. Prickly pears are as versatile as other fruits and can be served and used in countless ways. And you can do as many things with *nopalitos* as you can with green beans or okra, two vegetables they resemble.

Cooking with Nopalitos

Most commercial *nopalitos,* those sold in markets, are gathered from the domesticated *Opuntia ficus-indica,* a native of Mexico; *Opuntia basilaris,* beaver's tail cactus; or a hybrid prickly pear. But other opuntia stems can be eaten, too. Harvest them in spring and take only the young pads or joints. Old stems will be tough and stringy. If you are careful not to injure the plant, growth will begin again where you remove the stems.

Whether you are using canned or fresh *nopalitos,* there are many fascinating ways to serve them. They are good served plain with butter and salt and pepper or with a good chili sauce. They can be added to dips, supper dishes and casseroles, tacos, and omelets. And they combine well with many salad ingredients, particularly lettuce, cabbage, celery, tomatoes, onions, avocados, pimientos, green peppers, and a number of beans. The Mexican Indians sprinkle them over beans for crunchiness.

Prickly pear opuntia

PREPARING THE STEMS If you are lucky enough to have a source of fresh *nopalitos,* you will have to despine them before using. One method used by Indians was to boil them off. This method leads to overcooking and is not helpful if you want to eat the *nopalitos* raw. But blanching (parboiling briefly) will tenderize the spines and make despining easier.

Nopalitos

Modern cooks favor brushing spines away or removing them with a paring knife or potato peeler:
1. Hold the stem with tongs.
2. Cut out spines with a sharp paring knife or pull out with tweezers, being sure to get entire areole.
3. Brush away glochids (finer spines) with a firm brush or singe off over a flame.
4. Wash and drain.

The stems are now ready to use or cook.
To use raw:
1. Soak in salt water for several hours. (They will keep up to two weeks if stored covered in the refrigerator.)
2. Rinse, drain, and dice or slice.

To prepare cooked nopalitos *or* nopalitos tiernos (nopalitos *cooked tender):*

1. Cut the stems to the size you want. (*Nopalitos tiernos* are generally diced or cut into shoestring strips.)

2. Boil in salted water until tender, five to twenty minutes. (Add onion or garlic for flavor, if you like. Use about a quart of water and a teaspoon of salt for every two cups of prepared stems. Length of cooking depends on the degree of tenderness you prefer and the size and age of the stems.)

3. When pads are cooked, they become mucilaginous (gooey). Drain and rinse in cool water until stickiness is removed.

NOPALITOS GUACAMOLE DIP

Makes one to one and one-half cups of dip.

1 medium to large ripe avocado, peeled and pitted
¼ cup onion, minced
¾ cups marinated or pickled *nopalitos,* drained
1 small tomato, peeled and drained

1 tablespoon mayonnaise
1 teaspoon lemon juice
Salt and pepper to taste
Dash of Tabasco sauce (optional)
Corn chips, tortilla chips, or vegetable slices

1. Mash the avocado in a bowl until it is smooth and free of lumps.

2. Add the remaining ingredients (except chips) and mix well or put through a blender.

3. Put in a serving dish and serve with corn or tortilla chips or slices of raw vegetables (celery, carrots, green onions, cauliflower, bell pepper, zucchini).

Note: To peel tomato, drop gently in boiling water for one minute. Remove with a fork or tongs and dip in a bowl of cold water. The peeling will now come off easily with a paring knife.

SOUTHWESTERN GREEN SALAD

Chill *nopalitos tiernos,* fresh or canned. Rinse and drain. Or use *Nopalitos en Escabeche,* drained. Add to any tossed green salad, about two tablespoons per serving, and top with your favorite salad dressing. Garnish with tomato wedges, strips of cheese, anchovies, or strips of pimiento.

Variation: In place of cooked or pickled *nopalitos,* add raw ones which have been peeled and soaked in salt water, drained, and cut into slim shreds.

THREE BEANS PLUS ONE SALAD

Serves six to eight.

1 cup canned kidney beans, drained
1 cup canned wax beans, drained
1 cup canned green beans, drained
1 cup marinated or pickled *nopalitos,*
  drained

½ cup bell pepper, cut into thin rings
½ cup red pepper, cut into thin rings
¼ cup onion, cut into thin rings
Salt and pepper to taste
Sweet dressing (below)

1. Combine vegetables in a large bowl and turn thoroughly.
2. Prepare dressing and pour over the vegetable mixture.
3. Cover and chill in refrigerator at least six hours.
4. Serve on a bed of lettuce. Garnish with pimiento stuffed olives and slices of pimiento.

Sweet salad dressing: Combine ¼ cup each olive or salad oil, vinegar, and sugar. Shake vigorously in a covered jar.

Variation: In place of one of the beans listed above, substitute one cup of garbanzo beans, drained.

NOPALITOS GREEN PEPPER CHEESE SALAD

Served with hunks of good bread, warm tortillas, or crackers, this makes a light lunch. Serves three to four.

---

2 cups raw or cooked *nopalitos,* rinsed and drained
1 cup bell pepper, diced
1 cup cheddar cheese, cut into small cubes

2 tablespoons onion, chopped
⅛ teaspoon sage (optional)
Lettuce leaves
Tomato wedges and hardboiled eggs (optional)
Salad dressing

1. Mix *nopalitos,* green pepper, cheese, onion, and sage in a bowl and set in refrigerator to chill.
2. Arrange over lettuce leaves on individual plates and top with a tangy dressing. Garnish with tomato wedges and hardboiled eggs.

FRIED NOPALITOS

In Mexico *nopalitos* are often dipped in cornmeal and fried. Do that or try these batter-fried cactus stems.

Prepared raw *nopalitos,* cut in quarters
1 cup egg
1 cup milk

Salt and pepper to taste
Cracker crumbs
Butter

1. Prepare the *nopalitos.*
2. Beat egg with milk and salt and pepper.
3. Dip *nopalitos* in batter and roll in cracker crumbs.
4. Dip in batter again and fry in butter until cracker crumbs become crisp and brown.
5. Serve hot.

NOPALITOS CHINESE

Serves four to six.

2 cups prepared raw *nopalitos,* cut in quarters or thick slices
½ cup bacon fat or oil

2 tablespoons chopped onion
3 tablespoons vinegar
3 tablespoons sugar

1. Prepare the *nopalitos.*
2. Heat fat or oil in a heavy skillet and fry *nopalitos* until crisp. Drain on paper towels.
3. Pour off all but two or three tablespoons fat and fry chopped onions until transparent.
4. Return *nopalitos* to skillet and add vinegar and sugar.
5. Stir until heated through and sugar is dissolved.
6. Serve plain or topped with crumbled bits of bacon.

NOPALITOS AND EGGS

Serves three to four.

2 tablespoons butter, oil, or bacon fat
½ to 1 cup *nopalitos tiernos,* rinsed and drained
⅛ cup onion, minced

6 eggs, beaten slightly
Salt and pepper to taste
½ teaspoon chili powder (optional)
Bacon (optional)

1. Heat butter in heavy frying pan and sauté onions until golden brown.
2. Add *nopalitos* and cook until heated through.
3. Add eggs and spices and scramble lightly.
4. Serve plain or garnish with bits of bacon.

SPAGHETTI SAUCE RIO GRANDE

Serves six to eight.

---

2 tablespoons vegetable oil
1 medium onion, chopped
1 clove garlic, minced
1 bell pepper, chopped
1 cup *nopalitos,* diced and drained
1 pound lean ground beef
Salt and pepper to taste

1 bay leaf
1 teaspoon oregano
1 tablespoon chili powder
2 cups (one 16-ounce can tomatoes)
2 cups (one 16-ounce can tomato puree)
Spaghetti or rice

1. Heat vegetable oil in a heavy skillet or pan and sauté onion and garlic until golden brown.
2. Add bell pepper and *nopalitos* and cook until vegetables begin to soften.
3. Add meat and cook until it loses its redness.
4. Add remaining ingredients and simmer gently for 45 minutes, stirring occasionally. Add water, if necessary, during cooking to keep sauce from sticking or getting too thick.
5. Serve over cooked spaghetti or mix with cooked rice. Top with grated cheddar cheese, if you like, or chopped pepper, radishes, or fresh *nopalitos.*

NOPALITOS BEEF DINNER WITH DUMPLINGS

Serves four to six.

---

2 tablespoons oil
½ cup onion, chopped
1½ pounds ground beef
1 can (26 ounces) condensed vegetable
  soup

½ cup celery, sliced
1 cup *nopalitos,* diced and drained
Salt and pepper to taste
1 tablespoon chili powder (optional)
2 cups Bisquick baking mix

1 large potato, pared and diced
1½ cups water

⅔ cup milk
Parsley sprigs

1. Heat oil in a Dutch oven and brown onion.
2. Add ground beef and cook until redness is gone. Drain off excess grease.
3. Stir in soup, potato, water, celery, *nopalitos,* salt, and spices and heat to boiling. Reduce heat and simmer covered for 20 minutes.
4. Meanwhile, add milk to Bisquick and mix to a soft dough.
5. Drop by spoonfuls onto beef mixture. Cook uncovered over low heat 10 minutes.
6. Cover and cook 10 minutes longer.
7. Garnish with parsley and serve.

Cooking and Eating Prickly Pears

In Mexico, prickly pears are quite popular. They are sold in most markets and in some places are stuck on yucca leaves and sold on street corners. Prickly pears are also popular in Spain and Sicily. In the United States, prickly pears are most popular among the Mexican families of the Southwest. Many families grow large prickly pears in their yards.

Prickly pears are delicious eaten raw, with or without seeds, and also can be cooked in various ways. Before you can eat or use them, they must be rid of their spines and peelings.

Fruit from domesticated cacti are good. But many native species produce good fruit, too. *Opuntia phaecantha,* Engelmann's prickly pear, and *Opuntia linguiformis* are widely used, especially for jelly and candy making.

PREPARING THE FRUIT An Indian method of despining cactus fruits was to roll them back and forth over sandy soil with a broom of yucca leaf fibers or to shake them in a mesh bag until the spines came off. This is still a good method if you are on a hike and have no tools. Kitchen cooks will prefer the following method which is less likely to bruise the fruits.

1. Hold the fruit with tongs and knock off spines with a sharp paring knife.
2. Brush away glochids.
3. Wash.
4. Cut about one-quarter inch from each end of the fruit with a paring knife.
5. Slit skin carefully in segments from the small end to the large end and peel back the skin, which should take along the areoles.

The prepared fruit is now ready to eat as is or use in cooking. Fresh prickly pears are usually eaten seeds and all, though you can remove the seeds first if you don't mind losing half the pulp.

To seed, slit the fruit open and scrape out the seeds and inner pulp with a spoon.

To puree cactus fruits, prepare fruits by despining and peeling. Then force the pulp through a wire strainer or food mill. This will remove the seeds and fibers. One large prickly pear will yield one-quarter to one-third cup of puree. The puree may be frozen until ready to use.

FRESH PRICKLY PEAR

Peel the fruit and slice in half. Squeeze fresh lemon or lime juice over it and sprinkle with powdered sugar.

This makes a refreshing salad, snack, or breakfast treat. To serve as a dessert, top with whipped cream.

PRICKLY PEAR FRUIT SALAD

You can add prickly pears to just about any fruit salad. They are especially attractive when sliced and used to decorate the top. The following is a tasty combination. Serves six.

1 pear or apple, quartered and sliced thin
1 small banana, sliced thin
1 orange, peeled, seeded, and sectioned
¼ cup raisins

1 stalk celery, sliced thin
4 to 6 prickly pears, peeled and sliced
Whipped cream, creamy mayonnaise
    dressing, or yogurt

1. Mix the pear or apple, banana, orange, raisins, and celery in a bowl and chill. Chill the prickly pears separately.
2. Just before serving, turn in prickly pears and mix gently.
3. Serve plain or on a bed of lettuce.
4. Top with whipped cream, creamy mayonnaise dressing, or yogurt.
Creamy mayonnaise dressing: Add ⅓ cup whipped cream to 1 cup mayonnaise and blend.

BAKED PRICKLY PEARS

Serves four to six.

---

4 to 6 extra large, ripe prickly pears
¼ cup sugar
½ teaspoon cinnamon

¼ teaspoon grated lemon peel
4 tablespoons butter
Heavy cream

1. Peel the fruit, cut in half, and remove seeds.
2. Preheat oven to moderate (350°F).
3. Lay the fruit in the bottom of a buttered pan.
4. Combine sugar, cinnamon, and lemon peel and sprinkle over fruit.
5. Top with dabs of butter.
6. Bake until tender, about 20 to 30 minutes.
7. Serve warm with cream or whipped cream.

CACTUS JELLY ROLL

This recipe is best with homemade prickly pear jelly, but any commercially prepared cactus jelly can be used. You may use your favorite jelly roll recipe or do it the easy way and use a boxed sponge or angel food cake mix.

---

1 box sponge or angel food cake mix
2 to 3 eggs (consult box directions)
Water

½ cup cactus jelly
Powdered sugar

1. Line a jelly roll pan or any shallow pan, 9 x 13 or 10 x 15 inches, with greased waxed paper. Cut the paper a bit smaller than the base of the pan.
2. Preheat oven to moderately hot (350°F to 400°F). (Check cake mix directions.)
3. Mix cake according to directions and pour the batter into the greased pan, tilting the pan so it runs to the corners.
4. Bake 12 to 15 minutes or until firm to the touch and slightly shrunken from the pan.
5. Meanwhile, spread a dry clean cloth on a work surface and sprinkle thickly with powdered sugar.
6. When the cake is done, invert it on the cloth. If edges are crusty, trim off with a sharp knife.
7. Peel off the paper, being careful not to tear the cake.
8. Warm the cactus jelly in a saucepan and whip to make it smooth and easy to spread.
9. Spread the jelly on the cake and then roll the cake the narrow way using the cloth to aid in the rolling if necessary.
10. Wrap in waxed paper until ready to serve.
11. Place on a serving plate, seam side down, and sprinkle lightly with powdered sugar.
12. Serve plain or with whipped cream.

PRICKLY PEAR SAUCE

A sauce made from cactus fruits can turn a plain dessert into something special. Pour over pound cakes, unfrosted white or yellow cakes, ice cream, canned fruits, and the like. Makes about one and one-half cups.

¼ cup sugar	1 cup prickly pear puree
1 tablespoon cornstarch	2 tablespoons lemon or lime juice
Dash of salt	1 tablespoon butter or margarine

1. Prepare prickly pear puree and reserve one cup. (See directions on p. 104.)

2. In a saucepan blend sugar, cornstarch, salt, and puree and cook until thick and clear, about 5 minutes.

3. Blend in butter and lemon juice and heat a few minutes longer.

4. Serve hot or cold.

QUICK PRICKLY PEAR SAUCE

Use cactus syrup, marmalade, or jelly as a base for your dessert sauce. Heat slightly in a saucepan and stir in powdered sugar to the consistency you desire. Add a touch of lemon or lime juice if you wish.

PRICKLY PEAR JELLY

Makes one quart.

---

2 cups prickly pear puree (See p. 104.)

1 cup water

1 tablespoon gelatin (1 envelope)

¼ cup sugar

Dash of salt

Lemon juice to taste (start with ¼ cup)

1. Puree enough prickly pear fruits to make two cups.

2. Soak the gelatin in one-fourth cup of the water until soft.

3. Meanwhile, bring the remaining water and the sugar to a boil. Add the puree and cook over low heat until the mixture is hot.

4. Add the gelatin mixture and stir until gelatin is dissolved.

5. Stir in salt and lemon juice. Taste and add more lemon, or sugar, if needed.

6. Pour into ice trays and put in a freezing compartment which has been set at very cold.

7. When the mixture is partially frozen but not solid, spoon it into a chilled bowl and beat until evenly blended with a rotary beater or electric mixer.

8. Spoon back into trays and freeze until solid.

9. Serve plain or top with fresh fruit or whipped cream.

PRICKLY PEAR SHERBET

It takes a long time to acquire the art of jelly-making. This recipe is included for those familiar with the process.
Makes three to four 6-ounce jars.

3 to 4 pounds ripe prickly pears   Sugar
Water   Lemon juice

1. Remove spines from the pears and slice the fruit.
2. Place in saucepan with a cup or two of water and cook over low heat until fruit is soft and pulpy.
3. Pour pulp into a jelly bag that has been moistened with hot water and let hang over a bowl until all the juice drips out.
4. Measure juice and pour into a four-quart kettle.
5. For each cup of juice, add one cup of water, three-fourths cup of sugar, and one tablespoon of lemon juice.
6. Bring to a full, rolling boil and cook until the jellying point is reached. (Fifteen minutes or more.)
7. Pour into hot, sterilized jars and seal at once.

Note: To speed up the process, add artificial pectin when you add the water, sugar, and lemon juice; boil three minutes; pack into sterilized jars. Consult package directions for amount of pectin.

CHAPTER SIX

Raising Cacti

Night-blooming cereus

Of all the plants in my home, I think I enjoy my cacti most. There is nothing like the pleasure of waking up one morning to find a bright blossom rising up from the spines of a mammillaria, a rebutia, or an echinocereus.

A famous horticulturist said, "Cacti are one of America's greatest gifts to the horticultural world." I think he was right. And so do many thousands of other plant hobbyists around the world. Cactus growing has become a hobby on every continent.

Cacti, of course, were not seen in Europe until after Columbus's explorations to the New World. Then they became of immediate interest to scientists and apothecaries of the day. By the sixteenth century, cacti had become familiar enough to be listed and described in botanical histories and writings. In 1770 the first expedition was made to the New World for the sole purpose of studying its plants. Soon after, businesses began popping up which traded in cacti and other New World plants. Aristocrats with large greenhouses began purchasing rare cacti and paying tremendous sums for them. Few of these plants came from the United States. Most were collected in Mexico and Central America, as it was not until the West was opened to scientific exploration just prior to the Civil War that our native cacti became known abroad.

Today cacti are available in most nurseries and commercial greenhouses. They can be ordered by mail from growers in such far-flung places as the United States, Germany, Australia, Mexico, and Japan. Many rare and exotic plants are sold as well as less rare and easy-to-care for plants.

Cacti are used as shrubbery and hedging throughout the Americas as well as around the Mediterranean and in Asia and Africa. They have become popular as ornamental plants in warm areas throughout the world. And they have gained great popularity among greenhouse and indoor gardeners. Though a rare cactus brings a huge price, cacti are no longer plants for the rich. There are cacti available today to suit anyone's pocketbook.

There are great advantages to raising cacti. They are interesting.

They are beautiful. And because they can withstand drought, they are well suited to the dry conditions of our homes. You can forget to water a cactus for days or even weeks and it will not die on you. And if you treat it right, it may last a lifetime.

This chapter will give you some tips on choosing and raising cacti. If you have a sunny room, your chances of raising a healthy collection of cacti are quite good. If you don't have a spot with a lot of sun, your chances are still good if you choose the right cacti.

Some Cacti for Beginners

When starting your collection, it is best to pick plants that are easy to grow. Once you have had some experience with these, you can begin collecting rarer or more demanding cacti.

There are literally hundreds of easy-to-grow cacti. And in general they require similar care. If none of these are available to you, ask the advice of your local nursery or consult a catalog from one of the mail-order nurseries. Most indicate whether a plant is easy to grow or requires special care.

You will often be given a plant's Latin, or scientific, name. This system of naming is described on pp. 153–155.

A plant that many people have luck with is the Christmas cactus, *Zygocactus truncatus*. It is a branching epiphytic plant. In nature, an epiphytic plant grows on another plant, but the *Zygocactus truncatus* will grow very well alone, in your home. It does not require full sun and can tolerate all kinds of soil as well. I have seen it blooming in the worst of conditions. To see its pendentlike branches drooping gracefully under the weight of its scarlet blossoms at Christmastime is a wonderful reward for any gardener.

Of the spinier and more typical cacti, for a first plant I would choose a peanut cactus, *Chamaecereus silvestrii*, a barrel cactus, one of the echinocacti, mammillarias, or echinopses. Most of these plants require a good bit of sun but are hardy and easy to care for.

PERESKIA ACULEATA
Mexico to Argentina

ONE OF THE PERESKIEAE Although few pereskias are sold in nurseries, they are generally easy to grow. *Pereskia aculeata,* the lemon vine cactus, or the Barbados gooseberry, has creamy lemon-scented leaves and a beautiful bushy appearance. It looks nice in pots and will fascinate your friends when you tell them that this leafy plant really is a cactus. It has yellow flowers and red fruits, but don't expect to see them. Pereskias don't flower well in cultivation. It is sometimes called *Pereskia pereskia. Needs full sun or light shade; lots of water during active winter growing period; likes humus soil.*

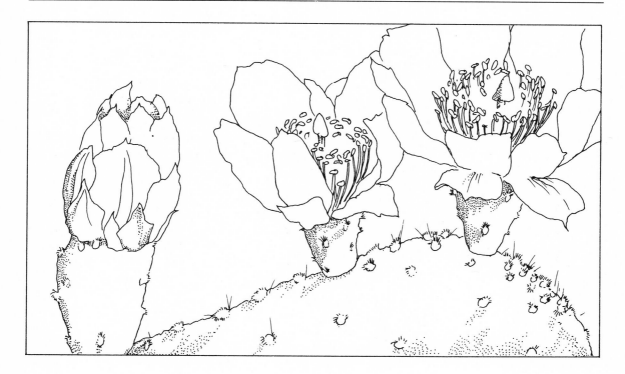

OPUNTIA BASILARIS
United States

SOME OPUNTIEAE* Most opuntias grow too quickly to keep indoors. They have a habit of spreading or getting tall in good light and rangy in poor light. But even so some can be used as windowsill plants. *Opuntia microdasys,* the bunny ears prickly pear, is a great favorite, and so is our native *Opuntia erinacea,* grizzly bear prickly pear. The grizzly bear, as its name implies, is covered with a thick mass of long grizzly spines; the bunny ears has perky, ear-shape pads which are covered by masses of luxurious-looking golden glochids. *Opuntia vulgaris variegata,* Joseph's Coat, is an attractive plant with smooth, multicolored pads of green, yellow, and white. *All need full sun and should not be selected if good sun cannot be provided.*

*The illustration above is a North American representative of this family.

CEREUS (LEMAIREOCEREUS) THURBERI
North America

ONE OF THE CEREANAE Of the columnar cacti, *Cereus marginatus (Lemaireocereus marginatus)* is one of the best-suited cacti to indoor gardening. It adds height and interest to any collection. It has erect, ribbed branches as do most cerei, and reddish bell-shape flowers. Don't expect the flowers, though. Most columnar cacti, though easy to grow, do not reach flowering size indoors. It is called the organ-pipe cactus but is not to be confused with our native organ-pipe, which is a different species. *Needs full sun.*

ECHINOCEREUS TRIGLOCHIDIATUS variety OCTACATHUS
Mexico and United States

SOME ECHINOCEREANAE The hedgehogs and their cousins are an adaptable and beautiful group of plants, many of which make excellent house plants. The hedgehogs produce some of the most beautiful flowers in the cactus family. Their ornamentally spine-covered stems form mounds or clusters 6 to 12 inches high. *Echinocereus pectinatus* is a roundish or oval plant, with prominent ribs, whose short colorful spines form starlike patterns. It has pink blossoms. *Needs full sun.*

The peanut cactus, *Chamaecereus silvestrii,* is one of the most popular clustering *Echinocereanae* and looks lovely in a shallow pot. It has small, short-ribbed, peanut- or finger-shape branches, weak but attractive yellow spines, and orange-to-red funnel-shape flowers. *Needs full sun.*

The crown cacti, or rebutias, are tiny, clustering, globe-shape *Echinocereanae* with ribs interrupted by rounded tubercles. Their flowers form a ring at the base of the plant. *Rebutia minuscula,* the red crown cactus, is a very popular spiny globe that produces a crown of red flowers at its base which nearly hides the tiny plant. *Needs half-shade.*

Lobivias are small, hardy, globe-shape or cylindrical plants which cluster at the base and produce flowers nearly as large as the plants themselves. *Lobivia wrightiana* is very appealing with attractive hooked spines, flattish form, and pale lilac flowers. *Needs full sun.*

Popular, hardy, and beautiful are the small, globe-shape Easter Lily cacti. Like their namesakes, these sharply ribbed cacti have long-tubed, showy flowers. *Echinopsis ancistrophora* has greenish-white flowers. *Echinopsis multiplex* has pink flowers and thick spines. It sprouts numerous "pups" from around its base when it is very young, which means you can propagate new plants from it quite early. *Both require full sun.*

ECHINOCACTUS HORIZONTHALONIUS
United States

SOME ECHINOCACTANAE The barrel cacti and their cousins are
easy to grow and popular with hobbyists. Many are free flowering.
The smaller *Echinocactanae* are best to begin with. Later you can try
your hand at some of the larger ones, ferocacti and echinocacti, for
instance.

  Echinofossulocactus heteracanthus, like most of the members of its
genus, will take a lot of neglect and will flower at an early age. It is
globe-shape and well supplied with round spines and wavy ribs which
give it the name brain cactus. *Needs full sun.*

Like most of the gymnocalyciums, or chin cacti, *Gymnocalycium damsii* is a free-flowering, globe-shape plant with distinct ribs that are notched into chin-shape protrusions or warts. Its blossoms are pink; its spines yellowish. *Needs full sun.*

If you have an eye for the bizarre, you'll enjoy adding an astrophytum to your collection. *Astrophytum myriostigma,* the bishop's cap, is a small, globe-shape, naked-looking plant with eight broad ribs dotted with white scales. As its name implies, it looks like the cap worn by bishops. It produces yellow flowers and blossoms freely. *Needs full sun.*

Most of the ball-like notocacti make excellent window plants. *Notocactus ottonis,* Indian head, particularly is fun as it matures and flowers at an early age. It is a bright green clustering plant with red-brown central spines and deep golden flowers. *Requires full sun in winter; some protection in summer.*

Parodia is a lovely cactus genus. Many are quite decorative with beautifully colored hooked spines and masses of bright flowers. *Parodia mutabilis* has orange-red hooked spines and bright yellow flowers. *Needs full sun.*

EPIPHYLLUM PEKOKIE
Brazil

SOME OF THE EPIPHYLLANAE The Christmas cactus, *Zygocactus truncatus,* is one of the tree-dwelling *Epiphyllanae* from the tropics of South America. It produces beautiful red blossoms in midwinter and is easy to grow, making it perhaps the most popular member of the cactus family. It is sometimes called a crab cactus because of the clawlike shape of its stems.

   Similar to *Zygocactus truncatus,* and another Christmas bloomer, is *Schlumbergera bridgesii.* Its stem segments are not as sharply notched.

   Both like partial shade in summer and a bright window in winter, a soil rich in humus, and darkened rooms at night just prior to their blooming periods.

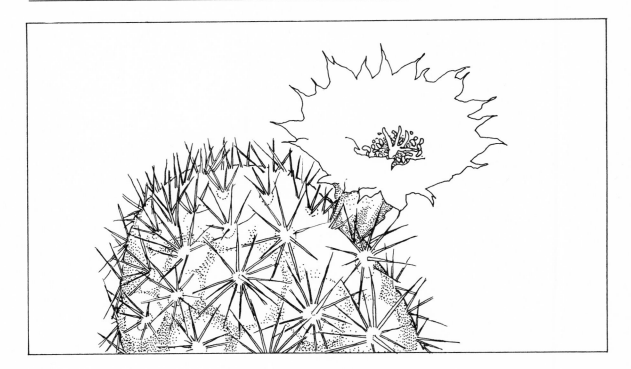

CORYPHANTHA VIVIPARA *variety* ANZONIZA
Texas

SOME CORYPHANTHANAE Subtribe *Coryphanthanae* includes the mammillarias, possibly the most popular cactus genus. Many of its other genera are popular, too. The *Coryphanthanae* are generally small and tubercled.

Thelocacti are noted for their decorative spines. *Thelocactus nidulans* is a semiglobose plant with large nipples, very long spines, and pale yellow flowers. *Needs full sun.*

Coryphantha runyonii, a hardy plant with short rounded warts, has a thick taproot and purple flowers. *Needs full sun.*

Mammillaria elongata, golden stars, is an unusual plant with many variations and can be seen in most cactus collections. It starts out as a small thumb-shape tubercled plant covered with a mass of yellow spines. As it matures, it begins to cluster and produce yellow flowers. It is a handsome plant by itself or in a dish garden. *Mammillaria mystax* is a perfect little spiny globe with neat pyramid-shape tubercles. Its flowers are rose colored. *Both require full sun.*

In general, you will have most luck with those species that don't get too big. The smaller cacti are quicker to mature, most apt to bloom, and better suited to windowsill gardening. There are exceptions, of course. But it is best to stay away from plants which are likely to outgrow their pots quickly.

Words of Warning

    Choose the most mature plants that you can afford. Young tiny plants in tiny pots are difficult to care for. This may seem to contradict the above advice, but what you must look out for are seedling plants or those sold in pots that are less than two inches across. Miniature pots cannot retain sufficient food and water to satisfy even small plants. If you do choose tiny young plants, place them together in shallow pots so that they will have a better chance of surviving.

    Check over all plants for signs of pests or disease before purchasing. Far too many nurseries sell insect-infested and diseased plants. Pots with green slime or a caked crust usually mean the plants have been improperly attended. Soil full of coarse, decaying plant matter contributes to cactus disease and may encourage insects.

Cacti can be bought at nurseries everywhere. Unfortunately far too many nurseries don't label their cacti. One has no idea what one is buying.

Where to Buy

    If you can't find labeled plants, you might order from one of the many mail-order cactus and succulent nurseries. They often advertise in the back of horticultural and garden magazines. Write for a catalog and price list. Spring and fall are the best times to order.

When ordering plants, ask for ones that have been seed grown or propagated from cuttings. They will be sturdier and cleaner than plants taken from the wild and you won't have to feel guilty about having taken a rare plant from nature.

Potting Your Plants   Think of its pot and soil as your plant's home environment. To have happy and healthy plants, you must use care in creating their home. An improper environment leads to disease, rot, or poor growth.

I usually repot all newly purchased plants to be sure they have a nutritious soil. Most nurseries use artificial soils which break down quickly. After the initial repotting, I repot again only when a plant outgrows its pot. The roots of a potbound plant will begin growing out of the drainage hole. Spring is a good time to repot, just before a plant begins its new year's growth.

THE SOIL   Cacti do best in a porous, fast-draining soil which contains plenty of mineral nutrients. In their native habitats most are accustomed to living in gritty soils rich in calcium and other minerals. All but the epiphytic cacti will like a soil full of grit and minerals.

Except for your epiphytes, soil which has a lot of coarse organic material will not be good for your cacti. Soil which forms a green coat or a white crust should also be avoided. The one would indicate that the soil is too rich in nitrogen; the other that it is too high in salt.

If you have only one or two cacti, you might simplify matters by purchasing a bag of prepared cactus soil for your plants. If you have a cactus collection, you can mix your own. The following are some cactus potting soil recipes you might use.

All-Purpose Cactus Soil Recipe

Mix:
1 part sterilized garden loam or top soil
1 part washed sand
1 part well-decayed leaf mold or humus or peat moss

To four quarts, add:

4 teaspoons of bone meal

3 teaspoons of gypsum

1 teaspoon of superphosphate

3 ounces powdered charcoal

3 ounces hydrated or horticultural lime

The bone meal is a slow-acting fertilizer. Some growers use well-decayed cow manure in place of bone meal, but used incorrectly it is apt to burn your plant's roots. The gypsum and superphosphate will assist in flowering. The charcoal will help to keep the soil sweet. The lime adds calcium which contributes to strong growth and blossoms.

Basic Epiphytic Cactus Soil Recipe

Mix:

2½ parts washed sand

1½ parts leaf mold or humus or peat moss

1 part well-decayed manure

To four quarts, add:

3 ounces crushed charcoal

Simple Epiphytic Cactus Soil Recipe

Mix:

1 part shredded fir bark

1 part sterilized garden loam or top soil

Simple Cactus Soil Recipe

Mix:

1 part coarse washed sand

1 part all-purpose packaged potting soil

Don't hesitate to adjust your recipes according to what kind of plant you are potting. The tropical and epiphytic cacti require more decayed plant material and less calcium (lime) than do the desert species.

How to Sterilize Soil

It is a good idea to sterilize any soil you bring in from your yard in order to kill any weeds, insects, or bacteria it may harbor. Dampen the soil and bake it in a slow oven (200°F) for one to two hours. Set the soil aside for several days before using. (Soil emits a strong odor when baking, so you might want to keep a window open and your kitchen door closed.)

The Pot

The experts disagree on which pots are best for cacti. You may use glazed pots, clay pots, plastic ones, or even tin cans. I prefer the look of a clay pot but plants do dry out very quickly in them. This can be an advantage if you live in a moist climate. If the air inside your house tends to be very dry, however, perhaps a glazed or plastic pot would be best.

Here are a few tips to follow in potting your plants.

Use sterile, well-scrubbed pots. Sterilize by washing in a solution of one part Clorox bleach to ten parts of water.

Use pots with drainage holes in sides or bottom.

For rounded plants, choose a pot which is only slightly bigger than the plant's diameter. A vertical plant will need a pot which is about half the diameter of the height of the plant.

Don't put tiny plants in tiny pots. Plant several together in a shallow four-inch pot.

If you want to slow down the rate at which the soil in your pot is drying out, sink it, or several, in a tray or larger pot which has been filled with sand or peat moss.

You can avoid a great deal of trouble if you provide your plants with good drainage. Place a piece of broken pottery over the drainage hole at the bottom of the pot to keep the hole from clogging. Cover this with a layer of pebbles or additional pieces of broken pottery.

Preparing the Pot

     Prepare larger pots this way:

Place a piece of crock over the drainage hole.

Fill the bottom of the pot with one inch or so of broken pottery or small pebbles.

Cover this with a layer of sand or gravel.

Sprinkle on a bit of charcoal and screened moss. (This prevents soil from becoming soggy and sour.)

Add a thin layer of soil.

Your pot is now ready for its plant.

Wear thick leather gloves when handling the cactus or handle it with tongs.

Potting the Plant

Remove the plant from its old pot by tapping it gently upside down on a corner of a counter or table. (The soil should be slightly damp so that it will come out easily.)

Position the plant in the prepared pot, being careful not to damage its roots.

Fill in with soil around the plant to the height at which it was potted before. Leave one half of an inch to one inch of space at the top of the pot to make watering easy.

Gently press down the soil and add more if necessary.

Cover with a layer of gravel, sand, or charcoal to prevent soil from caking up around base of plant.

Do not water the plant at this point unless you have been very gentle with it. Let it rest a few days out of direct sun to give any roots that might have been damaged a chance to heal. If you are sure no damage has occurred, you may water without fear, however.

Preparing
a Dish Garden

Dish gardens are popular ways of showing off a collection of cacti. They are often made to resemble a desert scene.

Good drainage is essential. You certainly wouldn't want your collection ever to stand in a swampy mess.

To prepare the bowl, fill it to one-third of its depth with broken crockery or coarse gravel. Sprinkle on a thin layer of crushed charcoal, then fill to within one-half to one inch of the top with a soil slightly heavier than you would use in a pot. A heavier soil would have a bit more garden loam and will hold moisture longer than a lighter one. Soil dries out faster in a wide shallow bowl than in a narrower pot. Sprinkle charcoal or decomposed granite over the top of the soil after arranging the plants. Add an accent of colorful rock or a piece of weathered wood.

Think of a dish garden as a temporary home for your plants. Repot when plants begin to get large.

Sunshine
and Temperature

The weather outside means very little to an indoor plant. Its climate is the sunshine and air within your home. Both are as important to your plant as the soil it lives in.

Most cacti are sun lovers and designed to take long periods of bright sun and dry heat. These cacti will be happiest if they get fresh air on a warm sunny windowsill during their active growing season (for most cacti, between spring and fall). An alcove window lined with shelves of glass is an ideal spot for cacti because its three sides increase the amount of time the sun is shining on them. If you don't have such a spot, choose the brightest window in your house and rotate your plants frequently to promote straight and even growth.

Even in the brightest window, your plants will not be receiving as much sun as they would in nature, so you might not get blooms.

But if they get enough light to promote good growth, they will be happy and so should you.

Plants which are not getting enough light will develop pale color and weak, elongated growth. If these symptoms develop, move your plants to a brighter spot. If you have no brighter spot, perhaps you should consider raising some of the epiphytic cacti which don't require as much light as the desert varieties. The orchid cacti, members of the Christmas cactus group, and rhipsalis do well in shadier areas.

In summer it is a good idea to provide some sort of screening, even for your spinier plants, to prevent sunburn. Pull a bamboo shade or a muslin curtain behind them during midday. If a normally green plant begins to turn red, this is a sign that it is getting too much sun.

In general, cacti will enjoy the warm spots in your house best. But they like lowered winter temperatures. High temperatures in winter can promote growth which will be weak because of the lack of light. Many people move their cacti to cool, unused rooms in winter to avoid this problem. The winter rest seems to promote blooming. Don't put your cacti in a room that drops below 45 degrees Fahrenheit, though, and your epiphyllums and rhipsalis will not want temperatures below 50 degrees to 55 degrees.

Though cacti enjoy fresh air and cool temperatures in the evening and winter, they should not receive climatic shocks. They will not take kindly to blasts of cold air from doors which are constantly being opened or drafty windows that get icy at night. Guard your plants from windowsill chill by plugging cracks with caulking and pulling a shade behind them after dark.

A VACATION OUT OF DOORS Most cacti benefit from spending part of the summer out of doors. If you have a protected spot to move them to, one with some protection from wind and sun, don't hesitate to give your plants a little vacation each year. Be warned though that they will need more water out of doors and you should check them over carefully for pests before returning them to their indoor spots at summer's end. Shade lovers will enjoy a summer "breather" hanging from a tree branch or in the shade of a grape vine, lathe arbor, or protected eave.

KEEPING YOUR PLANTS HEALTHY AND GROWING Cacti are hardy, adaptable, and able to withstand a lot of neglect. But that *doesn't* mean you *should* neglect them. Any plant is going to do best when given the proper amount of consideration.

WATERING Cacti need water just as other plants do. It is true that too much water will kill them. Overwatering is the most common way of killing a cactus. But don't try to imitate nature, either, by letting them go months on end without water. Even in the desert they get some moisture at night in the form of dew. And a potted cactus is much more fragile than one living in the wild. Its root system is weaker and can be damaged by prolonged drying out.

What's the answer then?

During their growing periods, from early spring to fall for most cacti, water regularly as the soil dries out. This will be every day for a few and every few days for others, depending on the size of the pot, the type of soil, the rate of growth, and the amount of heat. Test the soil by scratching it with your finger. If it feels dry, water the plant thoroughly; if it feels moist, do not water. (A plant about to begin new growth develops a lively look. Its head becomes a lighter green. It develops fresh white wool or new spines. Or new buds begin breaking through an old stem.)

Water your cacti on sunny dry days for the most part, not on rainy days.

Use water at room temperature. Cold water is thought to shock plant roots.

Never leave a cactus standing in water for any length of time. Empty your drainage saucer if excess water has passed into it.

In fall, your plants will begin to grow more slowly and new growth will stop. It is time then to begin preparing them for a winter's rest. Start holding back on their water. Where you might have been watering every few days, begin watering only once a week. Gradually withhold water until by the beginning of winter you are only watering once a month for large plants and once every other week for small plants. The exceptions of course are those plants which are blooming in winter, such as your Christmas cacti and the like. These may have a brief dormancy in early fall when you don't need to water as much, but in winter they will want their fair share.

As you begin withholding water, think about the room temperature your plant is living in. If you have it in a room which is very warm throughout the winter, move it to a cooler spot. You don't want to encourage your plant to grow at a time when it cannot get enough light, and there is no way it can get enough light inside a house during winter.

Set it back in the sun in early spring and begin watering more frequently.

Plants in pots use the minerals from their soil fairly fast. To put more nutrients back in the soil, you must fertilize. Cacti prefer fertilizers that are high in phosphorous and potassium. Most do not like those high in nitrogen. Ones manufactured for African violets and the like are not suitable for cacti. *Fertilizing*

Here are some guidelines to follow:

Fertilize your cacti once or twice a month during their growing season with a weak solution of an all-around house plant fertilizer. Use it at one-third to one-fourth the strength recommended on the container. Or use a small quantity of one of the following: superphosphate, liquid manure, or bone meal. (One teaspoon of bone meal is sufficient for a six-inch pot. Work into the soil and water.)

Do not feed your cacti during their winter resting periods. Overfertilizing can damage plants and cause them to die. The possibility of this happening is doubled during the winter when the plant is not growing.

Hygiene and Pest Control

A clean plant is healthier than a dirty plant. It will also be less likely to attract insects.

Syringe your plants occasionally on warm days with tepid water to clean off dust. Set them out of the sun to dry.

If you live in an area of high air pollution, you may need to bathe your plants with soapy water from time to time. Cover the pot and soil at the base of the plant with plastic, cloth, or foil. Hold the pot firmly by the top and dunk the plant a few times in soapy, tepid water. (Use a pure soap like Ivory or Ivory Snow, not a detergent.) Rinse the plant with tepid water. Set out of the sun to dry.

Inspect your plants for insects from time to time. Mealy bugs and scales are the most common cactus pests. Both are sucking insects. Scales have little flat bodies and appear as little flecks of paint. They can be scraped off with a fingernail or toothbrush. Mealy bugs are small white fuzzy insects which leave sticky cottony material on the plant. Spray these off with water and then touch any remaining insects with a dab of alcohol-soaked cotton. Repeat this process every few days for about two weeks to assure that you get all the pests. If mealy bug persists after this treatment, take the plant out of the pot and check the roots, as they may be infested with them. Plants heavily infested with mealy bugs or other insects may have to be sprayed with or soaked in a commercial pesticide. Use this as a last resort, however. Some cacti are sensitive to pesticides.

Separate any insect-infested plant from your other plants so the insects will not spread to your healthy plants. If you have tried everything and still cannot rid a plant of its pests, it is sometimes best to throw the plant out rather than risk the health of your other plants.

Special Instructions for Tropical and Epiphytic Cacti

The *Pereskieae* and the epiphytic cacti, *Hylocereanae, Epiphyllanae,* and *Rhipsalidanae,* can all survive periods of drought, but they do best if watered regularly. They all enjoy warmth, and except for the pereskias, prefer partial shade. Most will do best in soil rich in humus. For the most part, they do not require the winter's rest demanded by the other cacti. Treat them as you do other house plants and they will do fine.

Any good indoor gardening book tells you how to root cuttings and raise seeds. Basically you handle cacti in the same way you do other plants, with a few exceptions.

TAKING ROOT CUTTINGS Many cacti are easily propagated by taking a cutting or offset from a mature plant. You use a sharp knife or a razor blade to remove the cutting and you take it from a strong plant in the spring or summer. Then you let it heal or scab over before you put it in a rooting soil. The healing will take a few days to a week or more. Many hobbyists use pure coarse sand in which to root their cuttings, but you can use other rooting materials as well. Keep the sand damp but not wet. Place the cutting in a warm, lightly shaded area.

SOWING CACTUS SEEDS Cactus seeds will do best if sown in a sandy propagating soil. Three parts sand to one part finely sifted fertilized garden loam is fine. Add a little powdered charcoal to the mixture.

You start cactus seeds as you do any other kind, being sure to keep them warm and moist, but not soggy. Some cactus seeds sprout very quickly; others are very slow. But even a fast-sprouting plant will usually grow slowly once it sprouts. Care must be given as it grows not to keep it too wet but not to let it dry out either. Cacti, though tough when mature, are rather fragile as seedlings. Water with a spray or soak from below. Once the plants have developed spines, you can begin letting the soil dry out between waterings.

It is best to propagate your seeds during spring or summer when good light and warmth are abundant. When large enough to handle, usually within a year, move to shallow pots, several to a pot.

Whether raising a new plant or caring for a mature one bought at a nursery, you can learn more about it by observing it than in any other way. Let the plant tell you when to water, when to repot, when to start its winter rest, when to feed it. If a plant shows signs of beginning to grow, this is your sign to fertilize and water. If it seems to want to rest, let it. A person with a so-called "green thumb" is really just a person sensitive to the needs of his or her plants.

CHAPTER SEVEN

Vanishing from the Wild

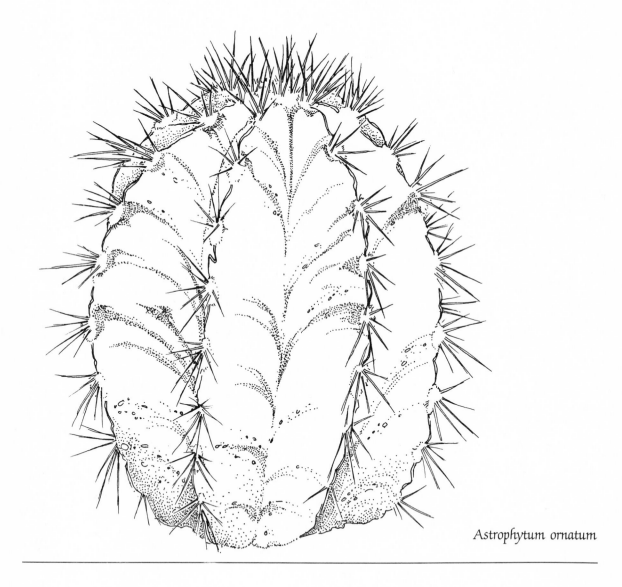

Astrophytum ornatum

*W*hat temptations we plant lovers face each time we visit a natural area. We find pretty flowers and we want to pick them. We find interesting plants and we want to dig them up and take them home.

Unfortunately, removing a plant from its natural environment can lead to the loss of that plant as a species. When we dig up a plant we are not removing just one plant from the environment. We are removing a seed producer with the potential to create tens, hundreds, perhaps thousands of new plants.

Plant lovers have caused the extinction or near extinction of a number of cacti. Either they have dug up the plants themselves or, by creating a market for rare cacti, they have encouraged commercial collectors to dig them up and offer them for sale.

Many cacti grow naturally only in very special environments. One species may grow on one mountain slope and nowhere else. You can imagine what would happen to such a species if a commercial collector came after it with a truck. As one botanist put it, "A collector could make such a species extinct in a few minutes."

Lyman Benson, an expert on North American cacti, believes that the cactus family may be the most endangered of all major groups of plants. He estimates that about seventy-two species, or 26 percent, of our native cacti may be facing extinction.

Cactus lovers have helped to create the problem, but they are by no means the only, or even the greatest, threat to these spiny plants. Habitat destruction endangers both rare and not-so-rare cacti.

Cacti are hardy plants in their natural habitat. Left alone in nature they can withstand just about any hardship the desert inflicts upon them. They have, after all, withstood drought, heat, wind, and the gnawing teeth of animals for centuries. But when people with their machines change and destroy its natural surroundings, a cactus is less able to cope. Once a desert or dry grassland area is bulldozed, plowed, flooded, paved over, sprayed with pesticides and herbicides, cleared, or otherwise greatly disturbed, cacti cannot easily regain a foothold.

You saw in Chapter Four that ranching is partly responsible for endangering the once common horse crippler cactus (*Echinocactus texensis*). Large areas of grassland in which this low-growing barrel cactus once grew are now used as grazing lands. Some have been removed directly by ranchers in an effort to protect the hooves of cattle and horses. Others have been killed because the grazing has changed the grassland habitat.

Grazing animals tend to eat grass down to its roots. Many grassland plants including the horse crippler do best in the shade of grass at least when they are young. Their chances of survival are lessened when the grass is eaten to the nub or trampled down.

Whenever people take over land for their own purposes, that land is somehow changed. Ranching, farming, factories, mines, roads, dams, power plants, and urban sprawl have claimed huge chunks of cactus land. Each has brought about changes which adversely affect all but the least sensitive cacti.

In the East we are accustomed to seeing our native trees and shrubs right in our backyards and along our streets. One is as likely to find a red maple, white pine, or birch in the backyard as one is to find these trees in the woods. These plants live with and around us. This is not true of most cacti. Certain species of prickly pear seem to thrive on man's alterations to the land, but plants like the saguaros, organ-pipes, barrels, and mammillaria can survive only under very special conditions. Change the soil, or the way water drains off an area, and the plants may not be able to survive.

In the cities of the Southwest it is rare to find more than prickly pears within the city limits. Maybe you will see a few lonely saguaros planted in brick-lined patches of earth outside office buildings or motels. And maybe you will find a garden or two where they are featured, but, for the most part, the native cacti are absent from the cities of the Southwest. You won't find them in the average yard. And you won't find them around ballparks, vacant lots, and other unpaved areas where native plants in eastern cities can often be found.

Is there any hope for our endangered cacti?

It is not easy to halt the flow of human events. The nation has been expanding westward ever since the Pilgrims first landed at Plymouth Rock. The demands on our deserts and drylands are likely to continue for some time to come. But there are ways to preserve that which we value even as we grow and, who knows, maybe the day will come when our appetite for land and resources will level off.

Most botanists and environmentalists agree that the surest way to protect a species of cactus or any other plant is to protect the habitat in which it lives. Preserves such as Saguaro National Monument and Organ Pipe Cactus National Monument are protecting valuable stands of cacti. Creating more preserves such as these in important cactus areas would be helpful.

Smaller preserves, too, could be created by local communities or individuals, especially if they adjoin other open areas. A thousand little preserves, if properly managed, perhaps could be as effective in saving cacti as one or two big ones.

Even such simple things as listing plants on building lots and trying to maintain the less common ones could go a long way toward preserving desert life.

Let's say, for example, that you bought a half-acre piece of land for a house. In one corner of that half acre was a nice group of barrel cacti and some hedgehogs. The rest of the lot was mainly creosote bush and gravel. Wouldn't it make sense to put your house in the open area and try to leave the cacti unharmed? Wouldn't it also make sense to design the yard to take advantage of these valuable plants? Instead of ripping them out and planting grass or marigolds in their stead, how much nicer it would be to include them in your landscaping plan.

Of course, this would be only a small savings. Protecting a couple of barrel cacti on one-half acre somewhere could not protect the species from extinction. But if everyone in your town thought as much about the cacti as you did, the savings could be great. And if everyone gave up the notion that life in the desert had to be identical to life in Virginia or Georgia, the natural things which give the desert its special character could be preserved for all generations to come.

In Arizona it is against the law to remove cacti in any area without a permit from the land owner. The Arizona Native Plants Law has given a certain amount of protection to cacti. Fair laws protecting endangered plants, if enforced in each community, could go a long way to halting the destruction of cacti. Stricter laws governing the behavior of people on public lands could help, too.

Have you noticed that there are rarely any plants in a barnyard? In areas where cattle congregate, plants get trampled down and soil becomes hard and lifeless. This can happen in deserts just as easily as it can happen in a barnyard. Desert soil is low in humus. It accumulates humus very slowly and is thus very slow to repair itself when damaged. Where cattle congregate in a desert grazing area, around a watering trough, say, the character of the soil is quickly destroyed.

If cattle can compact desert soil, it follows that jeeps, dune buggies, motorcycles, and other off-road vehicles can do the same thing. In recent years the deserts have become playgrounds for thousands of off-road vehicle enthusiasts. Motorcyclists and dune buggy owners especially have taken to the deserts in great numbers and can be seen driving helter-skelter over sand, gravel, rocks, and unfortunately, all too many cacti and other plants. Where they congregate, the desert soil has been compacted and many plants have been killed outright.

Riding the bumpers of the off-road vehicle enthusiasts has come another demon—vandalism. Many desert visitors bring with them the belief that the desert is a wasteland and therefore anything goes in it. Many seem to get a kick out of destroying plants. Throughout the desert you will find decapitated and wounded cacti. Barrel cacti attract the most severe attacks. Across the Southwest, large numbers have been hacked to pieces. In Arizona, the saguaros, too, have felt the brutal blows of vandals. Some have been carved with knives; others are riddled with bullets.

Why anyone would attack a plant is hard to figure. It is most likely done by the kind of person who in cities throws rocks at streetlights and windows or paints names on walls and sidewalks. The sad thing is that the destruction of endangered plants cannot be rectified with cleaning solvents, paint, or pliers. Once a species of plant is destroyed, it is gone forever. It is unlikely that any of the reckless desert recreationists who are destroying plants have any sense of the long-term effects of their behavior.

Gordon Rowley, an internationally known cactus and succulent expert, said, "Nobody can resist the cry of a suffering animal—a plant expires in silence, unmourned."

It is true that so far endangered animals such as the bald eagle and the whooping crane have received much more attention than have our endangered plants. But this need not always be true. Most people have a natural love of plants. They respond to the beauty of plants and want plants around them. Why else would there be so many gardeners? I suspect that the reason most people have not rallied to the plight of our endangered plants is that they are unaware of the problem.

Already, the situation is beginning to change.

APPENDIX

Though cacti grow in many nondesert areas throughout the Western Hemisphere, the greatest concentrations of these plants occur in the hot deserts and drylands of North and South America. What do these deserts have in common?

Basically, they are dry, windy, rocky, rugged places with little plant cover. Temperatures fluctuate greatly, humidity is low, the sun is strong, and evaporation is high. Rainfall is scanty or scarce in most deserts, typically amounting to less than ten inches a year. But that does not mean that deserts have no rain. Many experience huge downpours several times a year. But little of the rain reaches underground water reserves because the deserts' sunbaked soil is so dry and hard that it resists absorption. Rather than soaking into the soil, much of the rain merely runs off across the desert floor, collects in gullies, and rushes to low spots where it forms huge shallow pools. These pools dry up as soon as the sun comes out again and within a day or two no trace of water remains.

MAP OF AMERICAN DESERTS

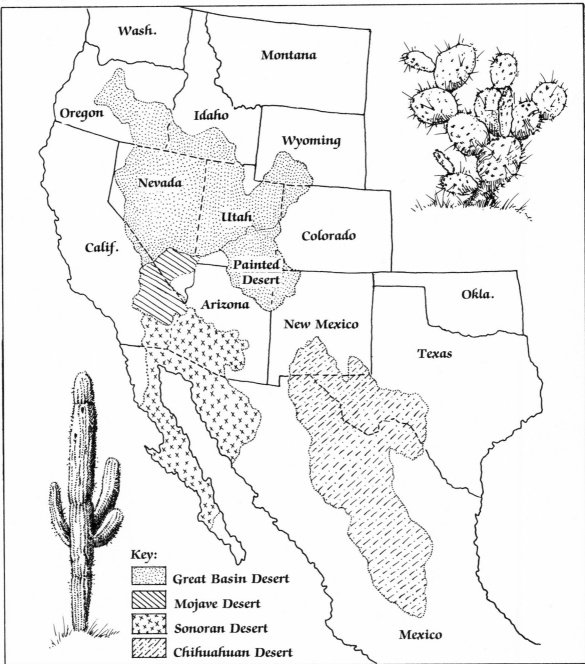

Wash.

Montana

Oregon

Idaho

Wyoming

Nevada

Utah

Colorado

Calif.

Painted
Desert

Arizona

New Mexico

Okla.

Texas

Mexico

Key:

Great Basin Desert

Mojave Desert

Sonoran Desert

Chihuahuan Desert

There are twelve large deserts in the world and three belong to the New World. The great North American Desert, which is about one-eighth the size of the Sahara, covers a large portion of the western United States and northern Mexico. It is divided up into six subdeserts, each with its own combination of animals and plants and its own set of climatic and topographic conditions.

NORTH AMERICAN DESERT AREAS

Four of these subdeserts occur in the United States.

1. The *Great Basin Desert,* so named because it is a series of desert basins falling between the Rocky Mountains and the Sierra Nevada, covers parts of Nevada, Utah, Wyoming, California, Arizona, New Mexico, Idaho, and Oregon. It is a high desert, occurring above four thousand feet in most areas, and is characterized by cold winters and mild to hot summers. It receives scant rainfall which is distributed fairly evenly over the course of a year. It is dominated by low shrubs, sagebrush, and saltbush, but it also supports a number of hardy cacti. The Charles Sheldon National Antelope Range in northwestern Nevada and Utah's Great Salt Lake Desert typify this desert.

2. The *Sonoran Desert,* which is probably our best-known desert, covers parts of California, Arizona, and Mexico. It is a lower desert with elevations below 3,500 feet. Winters are mild and summers are hot in the Sonoran, and it receives brief winter and summer rainfalls each year. Shrubs, cacti, and small trees dominate the landscape here and surpass the plants of other deserts in variety and abundance. Typical of the Sonoran Desert are the Saguaro and Organ Pipe Cactus national monuments of southern Arizona.

3. Lying mainly within California is the *Mojave Desert,* which is a transition between the Great Basin and Sonoran deserts and has some of the characteristics of each. It experiences cool winters, hot summers, and almost no summer rainfall. It is dominated by shrubs like creosote bush, but at higher elevations supports Joshua trees and a fair number of cacti. Death Valley and Joshua Tree national monuments are good examples of this desert.

4. The *Chihuahuan Desert,* which is located mainly in Mexico but which pokes up into Arizona, New Mexico, and Texas, is a high, cool desert, mostly above 3,500 feet. It is characterized by broad plateaus and winter and summer rainfall. Shrubs, grasses, agaves, yuccas, and some small cacti are typical of this desert. Exemplifying this desert is Big Bend National Monument in southern Texas.

DESERT GARDENS, MUSEUMS, AND NATURAL AREAS

Throughout the Southwest undeveloped areas along backroads and highways offer the cactus lover opportunities to observe cacti. Within the boundaries of the Mojave, Chihuahuan, and Sonoran deserts in particular, opportunities exist. Obviously, some areas are richer in cactus life than others, and you'll feel more comfortable in some areas than others. Not everyone likes to trailblaze. For people who want a clearly defined point from which to begin their explorations, the following list may be helpful.

In Arizona

Arizona is richest in cacti of all our states. A large part of the state is covered by the Sonoran Desert. Chihuahuan, Mojave, and Great Basin deserts cover smaller areas. (See map on pp. 142–43.) As a result, the opportunity for cactus study in this state is immense. As well as some marvelous desert preserves, the state has a number of very fine gardens and museums.

Arizona-Sonoran Desert Museum
Tucson Mountain Park
Tucson

Write to:
P. O. Box 5607
Tucson, Arizona 85703

A natural history museum adjacent to Saguaro National Monument with indoor and outdoor exhibits, displays of living animals, clearly labeled cactus and native plant gardens, and nature trails through several acres of desert vegetation. A good place to study the ecology of the Sonoran Desert.

Boyce Thompson Southwestern Arboretum
Superior, Arizona 85273

A thirty-acre tract of scenic Sonoran Desert beneath Picket Post Mountain adjacent to Tonto National Monument. This pleasant arboretum displays cacti and other plants from arid regions of the world. Contains greenhouses, nature trails through a stretch of natural desert, and a visitor center. Operated as part of the Desert Biology Station of the University of Arizona.

Desert Botanical Garden of Arizona   Write to:
1200 North Galvin Parkway   P. O. Box 5415
Phoenix   Phoenix, Arizona 85010

This 150-acre aboretum lies within Papago Park and is devoted to cacti and desert plants from all over the world. A lathhouse displays plants too fragile for the open desert. Self-guided nature walk, exhibits, visitor center. Founded and sponsored by the Arizona Cactus and Native Flora Society.

Organ Pipe Cactus National Monument
P. O. Box 38
Ajo, Arizona 85321

The National Park Service established this 330,000-acre Sonoran Desert preserve to protect the organ-pipe cactus and its habitat. Paved scenic drives, nature and hiking trails, information center, campgrounds. A wonderful place to spend a few days getting to know cacti in their native surroundings.

Saguaro National Monument
P. O. Box 17210
Tucson, Arizona 85710

An area of Sonoran Desert dominated by saguaro forests and established by the National Park Service to protect them. Paved drives with lookouts, nature and hiking trails, information center. Divided into two sections: The Tucson Mountain section west of Tucson protects 15,500 acres of young saguaro forest while the Rincon Mountain Section east of the city protects some 63,000 acres of old saguaro forest. The head-quarters and visitor center are in this larger section. Less remote than Organ Pipe, Saguaro National Monument is readily accessible to a large number of people living in the Tucson-Phoenix area.

Also worth a visit: Chiricahua National Monument, Willcox, Ari-zona; Picacho Peak State Park; Tonto National Monument and Forest; and stretches of desert along the Gila River. Backcountry wilderness buffs will enjoy visiting Cabeza Prieta National Wildlife Refuge and Kofa (National) Game Range. These two areas were established by the U.S. Fish and Wildlife Service to protect dwindling herds of desert bighorn sheep and Sonora pronghorns. Write the U.S. Fish and Wildlife Service, Box 1032, Yuma, Arizona 85364, for information.

In California

As in Arizona, there are many places in California where cacti can be seen and studied. A large part of the state from Death Valley to the Mexican border is desert. In the arid hills and rocky mountains running parallel to the southern coastline, you can find clumps of prickly pear, cholla, and barrel cacti. The hills around San Diego are dotted with cacti. And cacti claim spots among the rocks way up into Ventura County and above. But the easiest places to view these plants are in some of California's parklands and botanical gardens.

Anza-Borrego Desert State Park
Borrego Springs, California 92004

Anza-Borrego is the largest state park in the nation, having half a million acres of mountains, Colorado Desert, and badlands. It is a popular place for dune buggyists but also draws a number of nature lovers. Paved and gravel roads, backcountry Jeep trails, hiking and nature trails, camping, and interpretive programs. Look for the impressive stands of barrel cacti on rocky slopes throughout the park.

Death Valley National Monument
Death Valley, California 92328

Many people think of Death Valley as a huge expanse of sandy noth-ingness. Within its two million acres are wastelands, to be sure, but also mountain slopes and valleys with a wide range of desert vegetation including a number of cacti. Paved and gravel roads, Jeep trails, infor-mation center, interpretive programs, guided walks and auto tours in winter, camping, old mining town ruins, and a borax museum.

Huntington Botanical Gardens
1151 Oxford Road
San Marino, California 91108

It would be hard to say enough about the twelve-acre Desert Garden within the elegant grounds surrounding the Henry E. Huntington Li-brary and Art Gallery. It is probably the most beautiful desert garden in the United States. It is beautifully landscaped and contains an im-pressive collection of desert plants from around the world as well as a stunning array of cacti. Some specimens are the largest to be found in cultivation anywhere in the world. Don't miss the collection of mammillaria along the Center Walk. Guided tours available.

Joshua Tree National Monument
Box 875
Twenty-nine Palms, California 92277

This monument established by the National Park Service preserves a 557,000-acre tract of California desert. It includes impressive stands of Joshua trees, chollas, and other cacti. Paved and gravel roads, nature and hiking trails, information center, camping.

Living Desert Reserve
Portola Avenue
Palm Desert, California 92260

This 360-acre Colorado Desert reserve with trails and a visitor center features California cacti and other desert plants.

Moorten's Desertland Botanical Gardens
1701 South Palm Canyon Drive
Palm Springs, California 92262

A privately owned garden with a nice collection of desert plants and succulents from around the world.

Palm Springs Desert Museum
East Tahquita-McCallum Way
Palm Springs, California 92262

The museum features exhibits on animals and plants of the California deserts as well as displays on the geology, climate, and Indians of the region.

Quail Gardens   Write to:
230 Quail Gardens Drive   P. O. Box 5
Encinitas   Encinitas, California 92024

Naturalistic plantings of New and Old World succulents. The North American desert section emphasizes cacti and succulents of the Sonoran Desert. Guided tours for groups on request.

Rancho Santa Ana Botanic Garden
1500 North College Avenue
Claremont, California 91711

This garden features California native trees, shrubs, and wildflowers. Areas of the garden are devoted to the various plant communities found in the state with plants grouped together as they would be in their native habitat. Nature trails lead the visitor through these communities. The Desert Garden presents an extensive collection of California cacti and succulents. There is also an experimental garden and gardens showing how native plants can be used in landscaping.

Santa Barbara Botanic Garden
1212 Mission Canyon Road
Santa Barbara, California 93105

This sixty-five-acre arboretum displays California plants in natural settings. A small desert section is devoted to cacti and other plants of California's arid regions.

University of California Botanical Garden
Centennia Road
Berkeley, California 94700

A twenty-five-acre garden with a section devoted to cacti and other succulents, many from South America, and another featuring California native plants. Also includes an Indian nature trail and exhibits of plants used by Indians. Within the greenhouse is an impressive collection of cacti and other succulents.

The U.C.R. Botanic Gardens
University of California
Riverside, California 92502

Set in a rocky, arid section of the university campus, this thirty-seven-acre garden displays plants of California, collections of plants from different regions of the world, and a collection of cacti and succulents.

Also worth a visit: Barstow Way Station in Barstow, California, headquarters for the U.S. Bureau of Land Management's High Desert Resource Area; the desert lands around Inyo County National Forest northwest of Death Valley; Saddleback Butte State Park; the desert slopes around the Salton Sea; and the large expanse of desert along Highway 15 northwest of Barstow which is the site of the proposed Mojave Desert National Park. The Clark Mountains in particular hold some very valuable cacti and desert lands.

Both of these states can boast of broad expanses of Chihuahuan Desert
as well as other cactus habitats.

Big Bend National Park
Texas 79834

Big Bend is one of the most remote and unspoiled areas of the United
States. It is a blend of spectacular mountains, cactus-covered plains,
and desert wasteland. It is Chihuahuan Desert at its purest. The 708,000-
acre park contains paved and backcountry roads, an information center,
nature and hiking trails, and offers camping and nature study
opportunities.

Carlsbad Caverns National Park
Box 1598
Carlsbad, New Mexico 88220

This park is most famous for its enormous caverns, but it is also a
desert preserve of some 46,000 acres. Here in wide expanses of wild,
canyon-cut desert are many cacti and other desert plants. Nature and
hiking trails.

After visiting the park, you may want to cross the Texas border
and explore the desert wildlands of the newly established *Guadalupe
Mountains National Park*. Information about this park can be obtained
from the superintendent of Carlsbad Caverns National Park at the above
address.

City of Rocks State Park
c/o New Mexico State Park and Recreation Commission
Santa Fe, New Mexico 87501

The main attraction in this one-square-mile scenic desert park north
of Deming is the city of great stone blocks sculptured by nature. But
the park also contains a desert arboretum containing a variety of cacti
and other plants native to the Southwest.

Living Desert State Park
(The Zoological-Botanical Gardens   Write to:
State Park of the Southwest)   Box 1569
Ocotillo Heights, New Mexico   Carlsbad, New Mexico 88220

At this forty-eight-acre park overlooking the city of Carlsbad and the
Pecos River, you will see an extensive collection of cacti and other
desert plants planted attractively in curving beds. Other cacti are housed
in a propagation building, an entry building, and a succulent and cactus
pavilion.

Pancho Villa State Park
Columbus, New Mexico 88029

Within this park, established to preserve the grounds of an old fort, is
an outstanding botanical garden displaying a wide range of desert plants.
There are also trails through the desert, a museum, and a campground.

Also worth a visit: the desert regions around the Cornado National
Forest in the southwesternmost corner of New Mexico; desert areas
within the Rio Grande Valley, for instance around Bosque del Apache
National Wildlife Refuge near Socorro, New Mexico; the stretches of
scrub desert on the Edwards Plateau northwest of San Antonio; the dry
rocky areas of the Rio Grande Plain of south Texas.

Nevada and do Utah not have quite the cactus populations of the other **In Nevada**
southwestern states, but especially in the southern portions of the two **and Utah**
states there are areas of interest to cactus lovers. The areas around Las
Vegas are worth a visit as well as the Clark Mountains which cross the
border into California. Desert National Wildlife Range, a preserve for
bighorn sheep, and Valley of Fire State Park are interesting places to
explore. Edward Abbey, author of *Desert Solitaire* and other books on
the Southwest, found much of interest in Arches National Park in
southeastern Utah, including its cacti.

Outside the Southwest   For those of us outside the Southwest, finding native cacti presents more of a challenge, and we may need a botanist to show us where they are. However, there are a number of fine botanical gardens to fill the gap.

Brooklyn Botanic Garden
1000 Washington Avenue
Brooklyn, New York 11225

This lovely arboretum contains a very nice greenhouse collection of cacti and succulents from around the world.

Missouri Botanical Garden
2345 Tower Grove Avenue
St. Louis, Missouri 63110

This garden for many decades has been involved in collecting, raising, propagating, and studying cacti. Within its Desert House is a fine permanent planting of cacti and succulents and a rotating potted-plant display.

The New York Botanical Garden
Bronx, New York 10458

This houses a fairly large collection of cacti and succulents within its greenhouses.

Pa'u-a-Laka Gardens
Koloa, Poipu, Kauai, Hawaii 96756

This private garden is open to the public and displays a nice collection of cacti and other succulents.

Matthaei Botanical Garden
University of Michigan
1800 Dixboro Road
Ann Arbor, Michigan 48105

This university garden features an interesting selection of cacti and other succulents within its conservatory.

Water Isle Botanical Garden
Box 570
St. Thomas, Virgin Islands 00801

This lovely garden contains a sizable collection of cacti and other succulents.

Cacti can be found throughout the islands of the Caribbean. Especially in the arid backcountry, you should be on the lookout for them. There are heavy growths of opuntias and also some night-blooming cereus on the south side of St. John Island within *Virgin Island National Park*. Information about this park can be obtained from the National Park Service, Box 806, St. Thomas, Virgin Islands 00801.

UNDERSTANDING NOMENCLATURE: THE THREE CACTUS TRIBES

If you can't see a cactus in its natural habitat, a nursery or botanical garden is a good substitute. Most of the nurseries I visited in the Southwest carried a large number of cacti. They had plants from the Sonoran Desert as well as from Mexico and other parts of the Western Hemisphere. One nursery claimed to have just about any kind of cactus a person could want. I visited it and sure enough, there, growing in pots, were rows and rows of tiny cacti. Each plant had a name twice as big as it was. *Pereskia pereskia. Opuntia basilaris. Lophocereus schottii.*

Most popular cacti are known by common names like saguaro or organ-pipe. But to be properly identified all plants must have two Latin, or scientific, names as well. The names are put together something like yours and mine. The first is a sort of surname. It shows the genus the plant belongs to. A genus is a group of related species. The second identifies the species. The giant saguaro belongs to the genus, *Cereus* (sē'-ré-us).★ To distinguish it from other Cereus species it gets the name *giganteus* (gī-găn-tĕ-us). So its full name is *Cereus giganteus*. In Latin *cereus* means "wax" or "candle." As you can guess, *giganteus* means "gigantic." The organ-pipe also belongs to the genus *Cereus*. Its name is *Cereus thurberi*. Thurberi comes from Thurber, the name of the first person to discover the plant.

A number of plants also get a third name. A certain species may vary somewhat depending on its habitat. Variations of a plant species are called varieties. Such plants receive names like this: *Opuntia compressa* variety *macrorhiza*.

You don't have to know the scientific name of a cactus to admire it. But if you want to order one from a nursery or look up information about it in a book, it helps to know the Latin name. Common names differ from region to region and country to country. If used by themselves, common names can lead to confusion. A plant's scientific name can give you a clue as to where the plant fits into the cactus family tree, too. As you can see by their names, both the saguaro and the organ-pipe belong to the genus *Cereus*. This means that they are closely related.

All cacti are flowering plants and are thus members of a large class of plants called the Angiospermae. The angiosperms are divided into two subclasses: *monocots,* plants that develop from one seed leaf, as do grasses and daffodils; and *dicots,* plants that develop from two seed leaves, as do most broad-leaved plants including many garden vegetables. Each class includes many plant families. The cacti develop from two seed leaves, as you learned on page 51, and are therefore dicots. They make up their own separate family called the *Cactaceae* (kak-ta'-sē-ē).

The cactus family is divided into three subfamilies, called tribes. Each tribe contains a number of genera which in turn include one or more related species. (The word *genera* means "more than one genus.")

★Some horticulturists put the saguaro in the genus *Carnegiea*. Under that system of naming plants the saguaro would be called *Carnegiea gigantea*.

The three cactus tribes are the *Pereskieae* (pē-res-́kē-ē), the *Opuntieae* (ōp-pun-́shē-ē), and the *Cereeae* (sē-rē-ē). On the following pages you will be introduced to these tribes and learn something about the genera and species belonging to each. The saguaro and the organ-pipe belong to the same genus. Can you guess to which tribe they belong? You know that the most ancient cacti are called pereskias. The name of their genus is *Pereskia*. Can you guess to which tribe they belong?

The name of the main genus in each tribe is similar to the name of the tribe. How do you tell if the name stands for the genus or the tribe? An *ae, eae,* or *iea* ending tells you that the name designates a tribe or other large division of plants. Names designating a genus end in *a, e, ea, ia, oa, ya, is, ius, us, um,* or *ium.*

CLASSIFICATION: HOW CACTI ARE ARRANGED INTO GROUPS

Class: Angiospermae
   Subclass: Dicotyledones (Dicots)
      Order: Cactales (Cactus Order)
         Family: Cactaceae (Cactus Family)

Pereskieae (Pereskia Tribe)   The Leafy Cacti   **Tribe One**

The pereskias don't seem to fit into the cactus family. With broad, flat, succulent leaves which they keep throughout their lives, they seem like ordinary leafy plants rather than cacti. Their green stems are succulent inside but woody outside, and their flowers, too, are unlike those of other cacti. The pistil lies within the whorl of petals (calyx) rather than in a floral tube as in most cacti. How then can they be called cacti?

New stems, spines, and flowers all originate from areoles, those special growing points present only in cacti.

As you read in Chapter Two, it is believed that the first cacti were direct ancestors of the tribe *Pereskieae*. This makes the *Pereskieae* the most ancient of the cactus tribes and the closest link to other plant families. Each plant is a living relic of the past.

Pereskias can be treelike, bushlike, or vinelike. (See p. 114.) Their flowers grow at the ends of their stems or off stalks along the stems. Several may be clustered together on a single stalk. No other cacti have stalked flowers.

The tribe contains only one genus, called *Pereskia,* making it not only the oldest cactus tribe but the smallest. Most of the pereskias are natives of tropical America, though one or two species can be found growing wild in the southern United States. It is suspected that birds, or perhaps Indians, carried their seeds here long ago. (For example of Tribe One, see pp. 14, 114.)

Tribe Two   *Opuntieae* (Opuntia Tribe)   Prickly Pears, Chollas, and Fig Cacti

If a cactus has glochids, it is a member of the *Opuntieae.* All but one of the genera in this tribe sport those troublesome tufts of barbed bristles described on p. 115. Most produce other spines as well.

As a whole the *Opuntieae* is a tribe of many-jointed plants. Some grow treelike. Others are bushlike. Some grow prostrate or creeping along the ground. The joints of these plants may be broad and flat or cylindrical; they may be slightly ribbed, tubercled, or smooth.

In most species, leaves are present on the new stems of these plants, but these tend to be small and drop off as the stems mature. The most ancient of the *Opuntieae* retain leaves throughout their lives.

Wheel-shape flowers are common to this tribe. These never appear on stalks as in the *Pereskieae.* Fruit varies greatly among these plants, though in many they are large and juicy.

Members of *Opuntieae* are found throughout the Americas from the tip of South America well into Canada. Only one of its genera, *Opuntia,* has representatives north of Mexico, however. Fortunately for us, *Opuntia* contains more species than any other cactus genus—well over one hundred. A number of these grow in the United States. The flat-stemmed prickly pears and their close relatives, the chollas, belong to the genus *Opuntia.*

Some other genera in the tribe are: *Grusonia, Maihuenia, Nopalea, Pereskiopsis, Pterocactus,* and *Tacinga.* (For examples of Tribe Two, see pp. 63, 65, 67, 69, 71, 96, 115.)

Cereeae (Cereus Tribe)   Globose, Columnar, and Epiphytic Cacti   **Tribe Three**

With three to four times the number of cactus species found in the other two tribes, the *Cereeae* is a highly variable tribe. Its members range from giant cylindric cacti to tiny globose plants to flat-stemmed climbing or hanging cacti. These may be jointed or unjointed (composed of a single stem or several single stems). Many of the plants in this tribe are ribbed or tubercled or both.

With one exception, all the genera in this tribe are leafless. None has glochids. Most have flowers with very definite floral tubes. Most are spiny, though a few have just a hair or two in each areole. Because of its large size, the tribe is divided into eight subtribes.

Cereanae (Cereus Subtribe)   Column and Torch Cacti   **Subtribe One**

These are erect, bushy, arching, or diffuse cylindrical plants. Some reach giant proportions with several to many long cylindrical joints. Their joints are ribbed, and in some, tubercled. Most are very spiny. Their flowers appear at the sides of their stems.

A number of genera are included in this subtribe, among them: *Acanthocereus, Arrojadoa, Bergerocactus, Binghamia, Borzicactus, Brachycereus, Browningia, Carnegiea, Cephalocereus, Cereus, Cleistocactus, Corryocactus, Dendrocereus, Erdisia, Escontria, Espostoa, Eulychnia, Facheiroa, Harrisia, Heliocereus, Jasminocereus, Lemaireocereus, Leocereus, Leptocereus, Lophocereus, Machaerocereus, Monvillea, Myrtillocactus, Neoraimondia, Nyctocereus, Oreocereus, Pachycereus, Peniocereus, Rathbunia, Stetsonia, Trichocereus, Wilcoxia,* and *Zehntnerella.*

Subtribe Two   *Hylocereanae* (Hylocereus Subtribe)   Wood Cereus

Hylo is a Greek work meaning "wood." In the main these are epiphytic, vinelike plants which hang on trees or cling to rocks with the help of strong aerial roots. An epiphyte is a nonparasitic plant that grows on another plant. It gets its nourishment from the air. Another name for an epiphytic plant is "air plant."

Most of these epiphytic cacti have long, three-sided, angular, or cylindrical many-branched stems. They have small spines. Large flowers with long tubes appear at the sides of their stems.

Among the genera in this subtribe are: *Aporocactus, Deamia, Hylocereus, Mediocactus, Selenicereus, Strophocactus, Weberocereus, Werckleocereus,* and *Wilmattea.*

Subtribe Three   *Echinocereanae* (Echinocereus Subtribe)   The Hedgehogs

Echinos means "spiny." These are a very spiny, single-jointed group of globose or cylindrical plants, each less than twelve inches long. Spines in the group vary greatly though they are never hooked. Their joints are ribbed, these ribs often divided into swellings but rarely tubercles. Very few form more than one joint unless injured, but many branch at the base forming clusters of single stems called heads. As in the cereus tribe, their flowers appear at the sides of their stems. Their fruits are spiny.

Echinocereus, the principle genus in this subtribe, is one of the largest of the cereus genera. Other genera in the subtribe are: *Austrocactus, Chamaecereus, Echinopsis, Lobivia,* and *Rebutia.*

Subtribe Four   *Echinocactanae* (Echinocactus Subtribe)   Barrels and Stars

Like the *Echinocereanae,* this is a group of spiny, one-jointed, cylindrical, or globose plants. They, too, are ribbed. However, these ribs are often tubercled. Hooked spines are common to the group, and they bear flowers off the top of their stems on central areoles rather than at the sides, as do the echinocerei. These flowers tend to be small with short tubes. While the plants in the *Echinocereus* group never grow taller than twelve inches, some of the echinocacti attain great size and weight, though none get as tall as the cerei. A few branch at the base to form impressive clusters.

The principle genera in this subtribe are: *Echinocactus*, *Ferocactus*, and *Sclerocactus*, which are popularly called barrel cacti, and *Arequipa*, *Ariocarpus*, *Astrophytum*, *Copiapoa*, *Denmoza*, *Echinofossulocactus*, *Echinomastus*, *Epithelantha*, *Eriosyce*, *Frailea*, *Gymnocalycium*, *Hamatocactus*, *Hickenia*, *Homalocephala*, *Lophophora*, *Leuchtenbergia*, *Matucana*, *Mila*, *Neoporteria*, *Oroya*, *Pediocactus*, and *Strombocactus*.

Cactanae (Cactus Subtribe)　　Melon Cacti or Turk's Caps　　**Subtribe Five**

The *Cactanae* is a group of small globose or barrel-shape plants. Their flowers arise from special areoles located within wooly or bristly projections on the tops of the plants. Called *cephaliums*, these sit upon the plants like little hats. The plants are single jointed and have straight spiny ribs.

Two genera make up the subtribe: *Cactus* and *Discocactus*.

Coryphanthanae (Coryphantha Subtribe)　　Pincushions　　**Subtribe Six**

The coryphanthas are small globose and cylindrical cacti that are covered with tubercles or nipples. These grow in spirals, taking the place of ribs, and are separate and distinct from one another. Spines grow from the top of each tubercle giving the plants a pincushion effect. Flowers grow from unique growing points between the tubercles toward the top of the plants or from grooves on the tubercles. The plants often form large clusters.

The members of one genus, *Mammillaria*, exude a watery, sometimes milky sap, when injured. *Mammillaria* means "nipple."

Beside the genus *Mammillaria,* this subtribe includes the following genera: *Ancistrocactus, Bartschella, Cochemiea, Coryphantha, Dolichothele, Escobaria, Mamillopsis, Neobesseya, Neolloydia, Pelecyphora, Phellosperma,* and *Thelocactus.*

Subtribe Seven   *Epiphyllanae* (Epiphyllum Subtribe)   Orchid and Forest Cacti

The epiphyllums are shade-loving epiphytic cacti known for their showy funnelform flowers. *Epi* means "upon"; *phyllis* means "leaf." These many-jointed plants have angular, several-sided stems or long, flat, leaf-shape stems. Because of the shape of their stems, some horticulturists refer to these cacti as the "leaf cacti." This term can lead to confusion, as the pereskias which really do have leaves are also given this name. Most of the epiphyllums are ribless and spineless, though some produce hairs and bristles. Their areoles occur in notches along the edges of their stems.

Among the genera in this subtribe are: *Chiapasia, Disocactus, Eccremocactus, Epiphyllanthus, Epiphyllum, Nopalxochia, Schlumbergera, Wittia,* and *Zygocactus.*

Subtribe Eight   *Rhipsalidanae* (Rhipsalis Subtribe)   Chain or Coral Cacti

Like the *Epiphyllanae,* the *Rhipsalidanae* are nonribbed hanging or creeping epiphytic plants. But instead of having large showy flowers, the plants are small with very short tubes or no tubes at all. Their fruits too are small. The plants are much branched and many jointed. In a few species, leaves appear on new branches, making these plants distinct from all other cereus plants. Though spineless, tufts of wool, hair, or bristles are present on most species.

A few of the *Rhipsalidanae* have a controversial history. Within the genus *Rhipsalis,* which is one of the most prominent of the *Rhipsalidanae,* there are a few species which grow naturally in Africa and on islands in the Indian Ocean. It appears that they have existed there since before

Columbus came to the New World. As cacti are New World plants and developed in the New World, how did these species get to Africa? The question has been a puzzle to scientists. One theory is that the seeds of these plants were carried across the Atlantic Ocean by migratory birds. No one knows for sure.

Genera include: *Acanthorhipsalis, Erythrorhipsalis, Hatiora, Lepismium, Pfeiffera, Pseudorhipsalis, Rhipsalidopsis,* and *Rhipsalis.* (You can see examples of Tribe Three on pp. 73, 75, 77, 79, 81, 83, 116, 117, 119.)

GLOSSARY

ADAPTATION   Adjustment of an organism to the environment.

AGAVES   ah-gay'-vees   Succulents with sword-shape, often toothed, leaves, that are arranged in rosettes like the leaves of an artichoke bud. Also called century plants. Native to the Americas. Belong to the family *Agavaceae*.

AERATE   To cause air to circulate through.

AERIAL ROOTS   Roots exposed to the air. Common on tropical plants which grow on trees.

AIR PLANT   A plant growing attached to another plant or object but not parasitic. An epiphyte.

ANGIOSPERMAE   angio'-sper-my   Flowering plants.

ANTHER   The part of the stamen that contains pollen.

APPRESSED   Lying flat against the stem.

AREOLE   ay'-ree-ol   Special spine-bearing areas on the stem of a cactus.

ARROYO   a'-roi-yo   A dry gully. A rivulet; stream.

ASCENDING   Arising at an oblique angle or on a curve.

BAJADA   bah-hah'-dah   Gentle broad slope which extends from the rocky base of a desert mountain out toward the floor of a valley.

BERRY   A fleshy or pulpy fruit with many seeds embedded throughout the flesh. Formed from either a superior or inferior ovary.

BONE MEAL   A gentle fertilizer made of crushed or finely ground bones. A source of phosphate.

BRANCH   A subsidiary stem arising from a main stem or another branch. An offshoot.

BRANCHED   Having branches. Separating into branches.

BUSH   A low-spreading, woody plant, generally smaller than a tree. A low shrub.

BUSHY   Like a bush, low and spreading.

CAESPITOSE   ses'-pi-tos   Stems growing in tufts or mats.

CALYX   ka'-liks   Outermost case of a flower; the sepals of a flower.

CAMPANULATE   kam'-pan-u-late   Bell- or cup-shape; like an inverted bell.

CANDELABRA   A large, branched candlestick. Branched like a large candlestick.

CENTURY PLANT   See Agaves.

CEPHALIUM   se'-fal-ium   A wooly or bristly development at the top of a cactus which bears the flowering areoles.

CHARCOAL   A black material made of specially burned wood used as fuel and for filtering and absorbing unwanted material. Charcoal suitable for indoor gardening can be bought at garden centers and pet stores.

CHARCOS   Man-made rain holes (Spanish).

CHLOROPHYLL   Green matter of plants which aids in making the energy of light available for photosynthesis.

CHOLLA   *Opuntia* whose joints are cylindric rather than flat and whose spines are sheath covered.

CLIMBING   Supported by clinging.

CLUSTERED   Growing together in a bunch.

COLUMNAR   Like a column. Formed or composed of columns.

CONICAL   Resembling or shaped like a cone.

COROLLA   The inner petals of a flower, usually conspicuously colored. Not the sepals.

COTYLEDONS   kot'-el-edons   First leaves of a seedling. The embryonic leaves in the seed.

CRASSULA   kras'-oo-la   Group of herbs and small shrubs, usually succulent, of which the jade plant is a well-known member. Belongs to the family *Crassulaceae*.

CREEPING   Growing along the ground and producing roots along the stem.

CREOSOTE BUSH   kre'-ah-sote   *Larrea tridentata*. Common medium-size non-succulent shrub with a pungent, tarlike odor found principally on poor soils and desert flats in northern Mexico and southwestern United States. Produces yellow flowers and cottony seed balls. Also called greasewood.

CYLINDRIC   In the shape of a cylinder.

DECIDUOUS   Not evergreen. Leaves fall off at the end of each growing season.

DEFLEXED   Turned downward.

DICOTS   Dicotyledons. Plants with two cotyledons or embryo leaves.

DIFFUSE   Spreading widely in all directions.

DORMANT   Resting; not growing. Many plants experience dormancy, especially during winter. Desert plants are often dormant during drought.

DROUGHT   A long period without rain or water.

EMBRYO   A living organism in the early stages of development; the new plant enclosed in the seed.

EPIDERMIS   The outermost layer of cells of an organ.

EPIPHYTE   See air plant.

EPIPHYTIC   epi'-fid-ik   Growing upon another plant or object but not a parasite. Gathering nutrients from air and moisture around it.

ERECT   Standing upright.

EUPHORBIACEAE   u-for'-bi-ay-see-ee   Spurge family. A large plant family with over two-hundred genera, its best known genus *Euphorbia,* includes some one thousand species, most succulent. Some of these, especially the columnar and tree types, resemble cacti.

FAMILY   A collection of closely related genera. Families of plants are grouped into orders. Orders are grouped into classes. Classes are grouped into phyla. There are fifteen phyla composing the plant kingdom.

FILAMENT   The stalk of a stamen which supports the anther.

FIR BARK   Bark of fir trees. Available at garden centers.

FLORAL TUBE   An elongated structure containing the ovary at the top of which is attached the perianth (petals and sepals).

FLOWER   The reproductive structure in angiospermae consisting of sepals, stamens, petals, and pistils, or some of these.

FRUIT   A matured ovary and its enclosed seeds.

FUNNELFORM   In the shape of a funnel.

GENUS   A group of related species possessing enough similar characteristics to be treated as a unit distinct from other units.

GLOBOSE   glow'-bos   Globe-shape.

GLOCHID   A sharp hair or bristle tipped with a barb.

GYPSUM   A source of sulfur found in sedimentary rocks and used for making plaster of paris and in treating soil. Sulfur is one of the nutrients necessary for healthy plant growth. It is a protein provider.

HEAD   Stem.

HUMUS   Decomposing organic matter—leaves, stems, roots, animal matter—found in soil.

HYBRID   The offspring of parents that differ in one or more characters. Usually made between two species of one genus or sometimes between two closely related genera.

JOINT   A segment or section of a jointed stem.

JOINTED   Having joints; stems that are segmented.

JOSHUA TREE   *Yucca brevifolia.* Prominent tree-size yucca common in parts of the Mojave Desert and extending to other southwestern deserts as well.

LEAF MOLD   A type of humus formed of decayed or decomposing leaves which have accumulated in some damp place and become mixed with gritty particles of rock and sand.

LEAF SCALE   A small, more or less triangular leaf often found on the surface of an ovary or flower tube.

LIME   A white substance, calcium oxide, obtained from limestone, shells, and other materials containing calcium carbonate. Used in making mortar and cement and in neutralizing acid in soil. Calcium is a necessary plant nutrient which aids in the manufacture of new cells and the growth of root systems.

LOAM   A rich soil composed of clay, sand, and humus.

MEALY BUGS   Oval-bodied, sucking insects, up to a quarter inch long, with powdery-white appearance.

MESQUITE TREE   mez'-ket   *Prosopis juliflora.* One of the common trees of the southwest desert whose long roots, sometimes forty feet long or more, enable it to survive during long periods of drought. Resembles a small apple or peach tree with finely divided leaves and spines.

MONOCOTS   Monocotyledons. Plants having one cotyledon.

NECTAR   The sugary solution in many flowers which attracts insects and is used by bees to make honey.

NITROGEN   An essential plant nutrient used in large quantities by plants. Present in the chlorophyll molecules and a component of all proteins. Responsible for the deep green color of healthy plants. Found in most all-purpose fertilizers. Also in blood meal, hoof and horn meal, cottonseed meal, fish meal, fish emulsion, activated sewage sludge, and to some extent in animal manures and bone meal.

NUTRIENT   An essential ingredient of life; a nutritious substance. Of earth's elements, seventeen are essential for plant growth. Carbon and oxygen are obtained from air. Hydrogen is obtained from water. From the soil plants obtain nitrogen, phosphorus, potassium, calcium, magnesium, sulfur, iron, manganese, copper, zinc, boron, molybdenum, chlorine, and cobalt. Because plants need nitrogen, phosphorus, and potassium

in great quantities, these are considered major or primary plant
nutrients.

NOPALITOS no'-pay-lee-tos   Cactus stems. From the Spanish *nopal,* the name
for species of *Opuntia.*

OCOTILLO oh-koh-tee'-yoh *Fouquieria splendens.* Unusual looking shrub
with thorny, whiplike, unbranching stems growing upward in a cluster.
Common throughout much of the Southwest. Belongs to the family
Fouquieriaceae.

ORGANIC   Coming from living organisms.

OVARY   Enlarged lower part of pistil containing ovules.

OVULES   Egg cells; structures which once fertilized become seeds.

PALOVERDE TREE   *Cercidium microphyllum.* Green-barked desert tree somewhat
similar in size and shape to the mesquite. In late spring blanketed with
yellow blossoms.

PEAT MOSS   Partially or wholly decayed bog mosses. Best potting mixture
is sphagnum type.

PECTINATE   Resembling a comb.

PENDENT   Hanging downward.

PERIANTH   per-ee'-anth   The floral envelope consisting of the calyx and
corolla.

PETAL   One of the flower parts, usually brightly or conspicuously colored;
one member of the inner perianth or corolla.

PISTIL   The central female part of the flower which bears ovules and later
seeds. Composed of at least one ovary, stigma, and style.

PLUMOSE   ploo'-mos   Feathery; hairs arranged along each side of a central
spine or hairlike parts of a feather.

POLLEN   The dustlike spores produced in the anther and containing the male
germ cell.

POLLEN SACS   Elongated cavities in the anther containing the pollen grains.

POT BOUND   Plant's root system has outgrown the pot. Becomes obvious
when roots begin pushing out through drainage hole.

PRICKLE   A sharp, pointed outgrowth from the superficial tissue or skin of
a stem. Structure not associated with the center of the stem.

PRICKLY PEAR   Flat-stemmed *Opuntias* usually with large glochids and un-
sheathed spines.

PROSTRATE   Lying flat upon the ground.

PYRIFORM   pyr'-i-form   Pear-shape.

RIB   A ridge or raised surface running vertically or spiraling and bearing
areoles in a row along its top. Also a woody rod which gives support.

RIBBED   Having external ribs or ridges.

ROTATE   Wheel- or saucer-shape; spreading widely.

SAGE BRUSH   *Artemisia.* Any of a number of odorous herbs and shrubs belonging to the *Artemisia* family. Found chiefly on the western plains and deserts of the United States.

SALTBUSH   *Atriplex polycarpa.* Low desert shrub which forms extensive stands across valley bottomlands in much of southwest desert.

SALVERFORM   sal'-ver'-form   Having a slender floral tube which expands into a flat or saucer-shape upper portion.

SCALE   See leaf scale.

SCALY   Covered with scalelike leaves or bracts.

SCRUB   A straggly, stunted tree. Bushes and shrubs growing thickly together.

SEEDLING   A young plant grown from seed.

SEPAL   One of the outer flower parts; one member of the outer perianth or calyx.

SHEATH   Covering; a tubular cover.

SHEATHED   Having a sheath.

SHRUB   A woody plant having several main branches rather than a single trunk. Generally smaller than a tree. A bush.

SPECIES   A category in classification between a genus and a variety, subdivision of genus, second scientific name; a group of plants or animals having in common one or more distinct characters and being capable of interbreeding and reproducing their characters in their offspring.

SPINE   In cacti, a sharp outgrowth, rigid, woody, or flexible and hairlike, arising from an areole. Thought to be a modified or transformed leaf. In general, spines are sharp, woody, or rigid outgrowths from the stem, most being modified stems but some being modified leaves or roots.

STALK   Any lengthened support of an organ.

STAMEN   Male organ in a flower consisting of the filament and the anther; bears pollen.

STAND   A standing growth of trees or plants.

STEM   The main upward axis (straight line) of a plant; supports leaves, flowers, and fruit and conducts water and mineral salts for food manufacture into the leaves and food back out of the leaves and throughout the plant.

STIGMA   Sticky end of pistil at the tip of the style; part of female organ that receives the pollen.

STOMATA   A tiny opening in the surface of a stem or leaf through which transpiration takes place.

STYLE   Central stem part of the pistil connecting the ovary with the stigma.

SUBULATE   sub'-u-late   The shape of a shoemaker's awl, flattened and tapering gradually to a point.

SUCCULENT   Fleshy; juicy; a plant with fleshy and juicy parts.

SUPERPHOSPHATE   Ground rock phosphate which has been treated with acid. A phosphorus fertilizer. Phosphorus, a primary plant nutrient, is necessary to good root development and influences plant growth.

THORN   Same as a spine but not interchangeable with cactus spine.

TRANSPIRATION   The giving off of water vapor from living plants.

TREE   A woody perennial plant with a single main stem or trunk that usually branches above. A treelike bush or shrub.

TUBERCLE   A projection or bump on a surface.

TUBERCLED   Having tubercles or projections.

TUBEROUS ROOT   A root having enlarged fleshy sections like tubers scattered upon it.

TUBULAR   Forming an elongated hollow cylinder.

VARIETY   The smallest category used in classification. Subdivision of a species.

VEGETATIVE ORGAN   A root, stem, leaf, or other nonreproductive part of a plant.

YUCCA   yuk'-ah   *Liliaceae.* Bold plants of the Western Hemisphere, stemless or with woody trunks, having stiff, sword-shape leaves. Also called spanish dagger. One, *Yucca brevifolia,* reaches tree size. See Joshua tree.

WOOLY   Covered with long and thick matted hairs.

SUGGESTED READING

Abbey, Edward, and the editors of Time-Life Books. *Cactus Country*. New York: Time-Life Books, 1973.

Abbey, Edward. *Desert Solitaire, A Season in the Wilderness*. New York: McGraw-Hill Book Company, 1971.

Alexander, E. J. *Succulent Plants of New and Old World Deserts*. New York: The New York Botanical Garden, 1950.

Balls, Edward K. *Early Uses of California Plants*. Berkeley: University of California Press, 1975.

Benson, Lyman. *The Cacti of Arizona*. Tucson: The University of Arizona Press, 1969.

———. *The Native Cacti of California*. Stanford, CA: Stanford University Press, 1969.

———. *Plant Classification*. Boston: D. C. Heath and Company, 1957.

Borg, John. *Cacti, A Gardener's Handbook for Their Identification and Cultivation*. London: Blandford Press, 1973.

Britton, Nathaniel Lord, and Addison Brown. *An Illustrated Flora of the Northern United States and Canada, Volume II*. New York: Dover Publications, 1970.

Britton, Nathaniel L., and J. N. Rose. *Cactaceae, Descriptions and Illustrations of Plants of the Cactus Family*. (Four Volumes in Two.) New York: Dover Publications, 1937.

Butcher, Russell D. *The Desert*. New York: The Viking Press, 1976.

Dawson, E. Yale. *Cacti of California*. Berkeley: University of California Press, 1966.

———. *How to Know the Cacti*. Dubuque, IO: William C. Brown Company, 1963.

Earle, W. Hubert. *Cacti of the Southwest*. Desert Botanical Garden of Arizona Science Bulletin No. 4. Phoenix: Arizona Cactus & Native Flora Society, 1963.

Graf, Alfred Byrd. *Exotic Plant Manual*. E. Rutherford, NJ: Roehrs Company, 1970.

Haage, Walther. *Cacti and Succulents, A Practical Handbook*. New York: E. P. Dutton & Company, 1963.

Haselton, Scott E. *Cactus & Succulents and How to Grow Them*. Desert Botanical Garden Science Bulletin No. 5. Phoenix: Desert Botanical Garden, 1979.

Hesse, Zora Getmansky. *Southwestern Indian Recipe Book, Volume 1, Apache, Papago, Pima, Pueblo, and Navajo*. Palmer Lake, CO: The Filter Press, 1973.

Hylander, Clarence J. *Wildlife Community: From the Tundra to the Tropics in North America.* Boston: Houghton Mifflin Company, 1966.

Jaeger, Edmund C. *Desert Wildlife.* Stanford, CA: Stanford University Press, 1961.

———. *The North American Deserts.* Stanford, CA: Stanford University Press, 1957.

Kirk, Ruth. *Desert: The American Southwest.* Boston: Houghton Mifflin Company, 1973.

Kramer, Jack, and the Sunset editors. *Succulents and Cactus.* Menlo Park, CA: Lane Books, 1970.

Krutch, Joseph Wood. *The Desert Year.* New York: The Viking Press, 1951–52.

———. *The Voice of the Desert, A Naturalist's Interpretation.* New York: William Sloane Associates, 1954.

Lamb, Edgar and Brian. *The Pocket Encyclopedia of Cacti and Succulents.* New York: Macmillan Company, 1969.

Larson, Peggy. *Deserts of America.* Englewood Cliffs, NJ: Prentice-Hall, 1970.

Manning, Reg. *What Kinda Cactus Izzat?* Phoenix: Reganson Cartoon Books, 1969.

Marshall, W. T., and T. M. Bock. *Cactaceae, with Illustrated Keys of All Tribes, Sub-Tribes, and Genera.* Pasadena, CA: Abbey Garden Press, 1941.

Nelson, Sharon and Dick. *Easy Field Guide to Common Desert Cactus of Arizona.* Tucson: High School and Science Supply Company, 1973.

Niethammer, Carolyn. *American Indian Food and Lore.* New York: Macmillan Company, 1974.

Olin, George. *Mammals of the Southwest Deserts.* Globe, Arizona: Southwestern Monuments Association (Now Southwest Parks and Monuments Association), 1970.

Peterson, Roger Tory. *A Field Guide to Western Birds.* New York: Houghton Mifflin Company, 1961.

Pond, Alonzo W. *The Desert World.* New York: T. Nelson, 1962.

Shreve, Forrest. *The Cactus and Its Home.* Baltimore: Williams and Wilkins, 1931.

Smith, Gusse Thomas. *Birds of the Southwestern Desert.* Scottsdale, AZ: Double-shoe Publishers, 1973.

Tate, Joyce L., compiler. *Cactus Cook Book.* Riverside, CA: Cactus & Succulent Society of America, 1972.

Underhill, Ruth. *People of the Crimson Evening.* Lawrence, KS: Haskell Institute, 1951.

vanLaren, A. J. *Cactus.* Los Angeles: Abbey San Encino Press, 1935.

Weniger, Del. *Cacti of the Southwest, Texas, New Mexico, Oklahoma, Arkansas, and Louisiana.* Austin: University of Texas Press, 1970.

INDEX